THE PSYCHOLOGY OF RELIGIOUS SECTS

A Comparison of Types

BY

Henry C. McComas, Ph.D.

Assistant Professor, Preceptor in Psychology, in Princeton University

Author of
"SOME TYPES OF ATTENTION"

NEW YORK   CHICAGO   TORONTO
Fleming H. Revell Company
LONDON   AND   EDINBURGH

Copyright, 1912, by
FLEMING H. REVELL COMPANY

New York: 158 Fifth Avenue
Chicago: 125 N. Wabash Ave.
Toronto: 25 Richmond St., W.
London: 21 Paternoster Square
Edinburgh: 100 Princes Street

THE PSYCHOLOGY OF
RELIGIOUS SECTS

To

MY FATHER AND MOTHER

WHOSE DEVOTION MADE THIS
LITTLE VOLUME POSSIBLE

PREFACE

This little volume is an outgrowth of two very different kinds of experience,—a number of years in church work and a number of years in a psychological laboratory. The church work covered very dissimilar fields: slums on the east side of New York, a fashionable church on the west side, home-mission churches, churches north, south and west. In this religious work practical success depended upon the ability to interpret human nature. A working basis for classifying different religious types grew up unconsciously. Some people must be reached in one way, some in another. A successful worker bases his efforts upon a successful classification of religious types.

A few years in the psychological laboratory brought out a supplementary truth. No two persons are exactly alike in their intellectual and emotional natures. The laboratory has many ways of measuring individual differences. One of the most fruitful branches of Psychology to-day is the study of Individual Differences. These are found in Attention, Association, Memory, Imagination, and, indeed, in every factor entering into human nature. The grouping of these differences into types has not yet been accomplished but promises to be one of the achievements of the future.

The connection between religious types and these fundamental differences in human nature is so obvious that no one can come into contact with both sets of facts without becoming convinced that they are bound together. That is, the differences which appear in the religious life of different denominations have their only justification in the differences of human dispositions and not in any divine preferences. Nothing is more necessary to-day than the proclamation of this fact, for the heart of sectarianism is the belief that each sect is peculiarly a divine favorite. When all religious people freely acknowledge that their differences are matters of individual tastes and temperaments the real barriers to church unity will be brushed away.

H. C. Mc.

CONTENTS

I. INDIVIDUALITY 13

Rembrandt's Genius in Portraits Based on Individuality of Countenances — Greater Individuality in Brains — Evolution of the Nervous System — Its Response to the Demands of Its Surroundings — Social Environments Modify Human Nature — Effects of Events in Childhood upon Later Ideas and Feelings — Individual Differences in Psychological Laboratories — Differences in Attention and Imagination — Necessary Individuality in Religious Thoughts and Feelings.

II. TYPES 23

Types of Faces — Galton's Photographs — Physical Types of Human Nature in Sex, Race, Nation — Le Bon on the French Type — Gehring's Contrast of Race Types in Music, Literature and Art — Differences Due to Span of Attention — Types Resulting from Physical and Social Causes — Some Familiar Types — Social Laws and Types — Religion in the Individual and Type.

III. RELIGIONS AND RELIGION . . . 33

Types of Religion Not Due to God — Pratt's Classes of Religious People — Their Reasons for Belief — Some Philosophers' Religious Types — Definitions of Religion — Theories of Origin of Religion — They Do Not Establish a Unity — Practical Gauge of the Presence of Religion — The One Factor in Common in All Religions — Unity and Diversity in Christian Faiths.

IV. THE SECTS 47

Popular Idea of Church Growth Combated by Census — Great Membership, Wealth and Activity of the Sects — Cause of Weakness in Divisions —

CONTENTS

Evils of Sectarian Divisions — Two Instances of Over-Churching — Results of Sectional Spirit and Activity — Rights of the Public — Causes of Genuine Sects — A List of the Sects.

V. THE MAKING OF THE SECTS . . . 61

The United States a Fertile Soil for Sects — Immigration — Old World Differences — National and Racial Differences — The Civil War Sects — Sects Arising from Church Administration — Influential Leaders — Sects Arising from Protests — The Spirit of Conservatism — The Pioneer Spirit — Revival Sects — Doctrinal Sects — Differences Due to Natural Religious Types.

VI. CLASSES OF SECTS 76

A Classification of Sects Based on Their Origins and Characteristics — How National Stocks Affect Religious History — People of Northern Europe — Lutheran Bodies and Other Bodies of a Like Type — The Negro Churches — Revivals Produce a Certain Type of Sect — The Doctrinal Group of Sects — Ritualism Appeals to Certain Types — Leaders of Sects Gather Followers of Their Own Type.

VII. NATURAL SECTS 89

Natural Lines of Sect Cleavage — The Calvinist Type — The Typical Methodist — The Baptist — The Unitarian — Professor Giddings' Types of Mind and Classes of Sects — Comparison of Classifications Shows Two Centres of Types — Many Influences Obscure Natural Types — Unitarian and Christian Science Types Contrasted — Corroborations of Types Seen in Church Expenses and Their Locations.

VIII. TYPES OF HUMAN NATURE . . 105

Ancient Explanations of Types of Human Nature — The Four Temperaments — Possible Physical Causes of Temperament — Pyschology and Classes of Human Nature — Malapert's Orders of Nature — Giddings' Classes — Three Natural Divisions — These Types Characterize Periods in the Life of the Individual and of the Race — The Impulsive, the Emotional and the Intellectual.

CONTENTS

IX. ACTION TYPES 116

Central Place of Emotions in the Religious Life—
Action Types—Instinct and Action—Imitation—
The Average Man of the Action Type—Appeal Made
by the Roman Catholic Church to This Type—The
Intellectual Action Type—His Place in the Church
Anomalous—The Impulsive Type—The Well-wisher
—Types Scattered Through All Sects.

X. EXPERIENTIAL TYPES 134

The Meaning of Experiential Defined—Emotions
Enter into Experience—The Worth of Life in Terms
of Emotion—A Classification of the Feelings—The
Feelings Depend upon Physical Organs—Sex and
the Emotional Nature—Biology and Sex Characters
—Temperamental Differences in Sexes—Sex Differences in Religion—In Boys and Girls—In Adults
—Sex Preferences in Sects—Suggestibility of
Women—Emotion and Suggestibility—Suggestibility in Hypnosis and Conversions—A Conversion
Type—The Unstable Emotional Nature of Primitive
People—Professor James on Emotion and Inhibition—Emotion Spells Youth—Types of Emotional
Nature—Optimist and Pessimist—Relation of Feeling and Thinking—The Origin of Dogmatism—The
Difficulty in Unlearning Religious Teaching of
Youth—The Virtue of the Bigot.

XI. INTELLECTUAL TYPES 166

Obvious Intellectual Disparities—The Attention—
Its Relation to Church Services—Quick and Slow
Thinkers—Their Range of Thought—Ideational
Types—The Visualizer's Imagination—The Auditory and Motor Types—Theology Is an Expression
of Religious Thought—It Must Underlie Religion
Itself—The Direction of Religious Thought Is
Guided by Types of Mind—The Liberal and the
Literalist—Their Religious Lives—Imagery and
Ritual.

XII. THE INDIVIDUAL AND HIS SECT . 186

The Three Great Types—A Characterization of the
Sects According to Type—The Adventists—The
Baptists—The Christians—Coloured Denominations—
The Christian Science Church—The Congregation-

alists — The Disciples of Christ and the Churches of Christ — The Dunkers — The Evangelical Association — The Friends — Latter-day Saints — Lutherans — Methodists — Presbyterians — The Protestant Episcopal Church — Unitarians — United Brethren — Universalists — Tabular Comparison of Denominational Types.

XIII. LEVELLING FORCES 203

Forces Which Level Down — Inequalities in Society and in the Church — The Public School — Social Pressure — Fashions — Density of Population and the Spread of Ideas — Education Makes Leaders of One Type — The Mood of the Times — Modern Scholarship Makes Agreement on Bible Doctrines Practicable — Humanitarian Sentiments Make Unity of Viewpoints — Spirit of the Times in Church Buildings, Rituals and Sermons — The Reflex Influence of Missions — The Y. P. S. C. E. — The Sunday School and Other Church Agencies — Opposition to Closer Approach of Churches Due to Their Officers — The Greatest Levelling Force Is Public Opinion — Public Opinion Fosters Certain Movements and Opposes Others — The Kind of Public Opinion Which Fosters Divorce Fosters Christian Science — The Need of Cultivating Public Opinion for the Spread of the Idea of Church Unity.

XIV. POSSIBILITIES AND IMPOSSIBILITIES IN CHURCH UNION 217

A Church of Thirty Millions — Unity and Federation — Reunion of Sects Made by Civil War — Closer Relations Between Sects of Different Nationalities — Racial Sects and Missions — A Catholic and Protestant Federation — Doctrinal Differences Not Insuperable — Church Polity Not an Impassable Barrier — A Comparison of the Natural Sects — Groups of Sects Closely Related by Natural Traits — First Steps Toward Unity.

XV. IN CONCLUSION 233

To Correct Some Natural Misunderstandings — The Real Purpose of the Book.

INDIVIDUALITY

WHEN we study the genius of Rembrandt in those wonderful portraits, which look into our eyes with the sorrows and yearning, the wisdom and wonder of lives whose rôles were played in the dawn of a new age, the conviction grows that the secret of the master lay in his discernment and portrayal of Individuality. We feel that we are in the presence of personality, not paint. This feeling is accentuated if portraits hanging near the master's are in the monotonous uniform style of so many portrait painters. How acceptable are the lack of symmetry, the presence of unflattering moles, warts, hairs and wrinkles in those old faces by Rembrandt! Though we have never seen the originals there is a feeling that these copies are telling the truth about the originals, and to alter the lines would be to misrepresent them.

Nor would it require much alteration to completely change their character. The turn of a line at the corner of a mouth, the darkening of a shadow under the eye would make as great a change in expression as the alteration of a letter makes in the meaning of a word. Such slight changes as these make the face of each man unlike that of his fellow.

A sculptor accidentally injured the tip of the nose on one of the busts of Shakespere. The shortening of the nose demanded a lengthening of the upper lip; with the disastrous result that the immortal bard assumed an irresistible Irish smile.

When the numerous features composing a countenance are considered, it is no wonder that trifling changes produce an infinity of variety in countenances. If a chart in craniometry is studied carefully, it will become very evident that the length of lines and size of angles which go into the making of human heads are so numerous and so capable of variation that Nature has ample means for producing original countenances and has no need to duplicate.

These external and obvious materials are comparatively scanty when the internal factors are taken into account. Every brain, like every face, has its individuality; which has its source in a maze of brain-tracts. It would be far easier for two trees in a forest to be exactly alike in trunks, limbs, boughs, branches, twigs and leaves than it would be for two brains to have the same brain-tracts, the same connections between sensory and motor cells, the same synapses. While large and general similarities everywhere appear, the infinity of microscopic differences between two brains is incomprehensibly great.

In connection with these physiological differences between the brains of individuals, it is interesting to note the way in which the brain evolved in the course of ages. In every age it was a case of "demand and supply." An organism needed the means for adapting itself to the requirements of its surroundings; and from its innate potentialities and the conditions of its environment it developed the required structure. This process may be traced from the simple jelly-like, unicellular animal life among the Protozoa to man. When life depended upon the formation of contractile tissues, and, then upon nervous tissues, to coördinate the movements of the contractile tissues, in these simple organisms the necessary structures appeared. Or, it should be said, more accurately, that the structures and functions appeared in many cases; and in these cases the species survived. Of course, there have been many forms of life which have disappeared because they could not meet the demands made upon them.

Each of the end-organs, the eye, the ear, the taste and smell bulbs of the nerves ending in the tongue and in the air passages of the nose, the variously shaped nerve endings in the skin, giving sensations of touch, pain and temperature, all grew up as animal life needed to receive information concerning the universe in which it was trying to live. Some senses developed earlier in the life of one species than in the life of another. Along with this growth of the end-organs and nervous system went a corresponding growth of the "centres" of the nervous activities, the brain. In early forms of life the sense-organs for hearing, seeing, tasting and smelling appear at the oral end of the animal. They are situated near the mouth, as it is always the end seeking food and pointed in the direction in which the creature is moving. This position of the principal sense-organs naturally brought the nervous centres, which received the sensory impressions and which coördinated them, into the same part of the organism. So the brain developed in response to the demands of the environment. This enables us to see why the various animal orders have such dissimilar brains and it hints at a reason why the human brain should vary so greatly.

Environment does not cease its influence upon brain and nervous system even in man. Here, too, the subtle hand of the creature's universe reaches in and shapes his being. No such obvious characteristics are evident in the difference between the brain of an Australian Bushman and an English scientist as between a bird and a fish; but the Bushman's brain is very different from the Englishman's; and his environment plus that of his ancestors has made the difference. We may look for many of the minute differences between our fellows in the influence of their several environments.

This is more obvious in physical environments than in social. For many years sociologists have pointed out how the characteristics of the mountaineer, the plainsman, the sailor, the farmer and the merchant differ. In our own experience we have noticed the effect upon our lives of a sudden change of surroundings. Thus, an unaccustomed altitude quickens the heart, an unusually warm, moist atmosphere enervates us, climatic and dietary changes affect the entire physical system. But such factors are by no means a civilized man's entire environment. Indeed, they are the things of which he is least aware. His environment consists far more in those things which engage his thoughts and demand his constant activity. His daily occupation stamps itself upon his life. If he leans over a ledger all day, he breathes less than a quarter of the fresh air he would consume if he were a mason or a sailor. His thoughts, like the muscles of his eyes, become accustomed to focussing on one class of things to the exclusion of others. He develops his own especial sort of mental focus. Body and brain become bent to the prevailing needs. As no two life experiences are exactly alike, no two human beings can be exactly alike. True, similar environments would tend to produce likenesses in human nature, and do so; but slight differences in the original disposition respond to similar surroundings in such a way that twins who have a very great deal in common physically, frequently show the most marked differences. In their case the environment which has surrounded them from infancy up to maturity must be reckoned with.

It has been shown that the thought-life of the child is the keystone which gives shape to adult thinking. The first impressions of the sea, of mountains, prairies, great rivers, or any of the wonders of nature, are the impressions which form centres for all succeeding thoughts upon these things. When the word "spring" or "pond" is mentioned, I think at first of the meaning of the word as it occurs in its context; then, if a clearer and larger comprehension is needed, I find a visual image of a certain "pond" or "spring," connected with my earliest experiences, will come into mind. This is a very common experience. Some recent research in psychology tends to strengthen the belief that the earliest impressions upon the mind run down into the thought-life of all later years. It is easy to see how a vivid experience will start a series of thought-complexes forming in the child-mind which will be his and his only for all time. A rather striking case is that of the man who had an aversion for horses. He felt that the bite of a horse was especially dangerous, and rather feared a horse's head than his heels. He spoke of his persistent aversion to an uncle, who had known him in infancy, and learned that he had been bitten by a horse when he was a very small boy and had always dreaded them. The recollection of the event had long since faded out, but the effects still remained. With many children, apparently commonplace experiences make lasting impressions. Henry Ward Beecher declared that he never could endure seeing anyone box a child's ears, as it recalled a certain experience in his own mischievous period. Lincoln's repertory of stories was filled with scores of homely and quaint incidents which lasted in his mind throughout life. Everyone is aware that this treasury of early impressions exists. Not everyone realizes that many of his likes and dislikes, and much of the colouring of his thoughts, come from this source.

So it may easily be seen how the home, the school, the play-ground, the work of each child give a touch to his personality. Each touch means a slight difference in the building of his thought-life; or, if we retain the physiologist's viewpoint, to the fashioning of his brain. Each experience of the years of plasticity enters into the fibre of his mental and temperamental being. It would not mean the obliteration of individuality if every human being on earth started with exactly the same native endowments, for so diverse are the experiences which enter into the separate lives of those living in apparently the same environment, both social and physical, that each would acquire characteristics of his own.

Of course, no such identity of natural faculties exists. Nature is anything but stereotyped. "We see infinite variability in the endless slight peculiarities which distinguish the individuals of the same species, and which cannot be accounted for by inheritance from either parent or from some more remote ancestor. Even strongly marked differences occasionally appear in the young of the same litter and in seedlings from the same seed-capsules." * With the higher and more complex creatures there is greater opportunity for these native differences.

One of the most important methods of studying these differences is afforded by the Psychological Laboratory. Since Wilhelm Wundt established his laboratory in Leipzig in 1875, his methods and ideals have spread to nearly every university in the world, with the splendid result that a new body of scientific knowledge has grown up in a generation. From the material accumulated in these many laboratories, an intelligent investigation of the great principles of the human mind is possible. Not the least important part of this "New Psychology" is that which examines "Individual Differences." Some one characteristic of several persons is studied in detail and careful comparisons are made. Thus, by means of the chronoscope, an instrument which measures time in terms of a thousandth of a second, an experimenter can easily determine how long it takes a certain subject to perceive a light or a sound and to react upon his perception. Or he may measure the length of time it requires to discriminate between two colours or sounds. This would give a hint as to the quickness of the subject's mental activity. In these simplest of experiments very wide individual differences appear. Some persons are longer in recognizing an object than others. Some are very much quicker in their decisions and actions than others. To correlate a large number of such peculiarities is one of the great tasks of the psychologist.

Enough experiments have been made to show many

* Darwin: "The Origin of Species," p. 8.

striking differences among men. For example, the length of time during which one may keep his mind upon a subject varies greatly from man to man. Not only does the time in which the attention dwells upon a subject vary, but the extent of grasp of the attention itself is very variable. One individual actually receives more or less into his mind during a given time than does another. The same landscape passing a car window before two travellers, will not be perceived in the same proportions. Each man builds his mind with the materials which the grasp of his attention allows. More than that, when the materials which have actually entered the mind are recalled, each one uses his own method of re-collecting. Each finds his emotions entering into his thoughts in a unique way. When several students were requested to tell how they recalled a certain event, each gave a different scheme of recall and each had his own feelings attending his thought. One recalled the event entirely in terms of emotion, another in visual terms, a third in visual and auditory, a fourth found motor elements in his recollection. Nothing, therefore, is truer than the Latin maxim "as many minds as men."

When the higher faculties of the mind are engaged, as in imagination and conception, the most vivid distinctions of thought appear. I have asked a number of men and women of education to solve a simple puzzle in mechanics. Each one pursued a strikingly original method of attack. That these people lived different mental lives despite the identity of university training goes without saying. Nor is it different with all men and women. Any simple test will show these differences. Elaborate matters of imagination show vast dissimilarities. Thus no two persons have the same thought concerning the world. To one the world calls up a map, to another a globe, a third thinks of foreign lands, and so the variety continues. It is only when each stops and recalls the salient facts known about the world, according to astronomy and geology, that anything like uniformity of conceptions appears.

What, then, could be more obvious than that each human being fashions his own religious conceptions? The idea of God finds its material in the early teaching or thinking of each soul. Around the central thought gathers a host of impressions. In the "association test" I have occasionally given the word "God." The first thoughts which came to the subjects were "church steeple," "the soul," "mother," and such dissimilar things. The central conception of God is, of course, very vague; and around this the innumerable associations cluster, giving their colour to the great idea. Only theologians who have reduced God to logical and verbal formulas show any uniformity of conception, and their colourless abstractions differ, unless they deliberately mould them in the same historical matrices. Among the people who are not professional experts in defining their conception of God, but whose lives are permeated with the inspiration of the thought of Him, there is a glorious profusion of differences. Indeed, where the figure of Christ is conceived as the great image of God, the innumerable likenesses of Him afford almost as large a field for choice of conceptions. Perhaps the thought which endeavours to make clear to the mind what is meant by God is no more individual with each person than the emotion which joins such thought. Here again the life-experience of each mortal weaves itself into his religious feelings. Love, fear, awe, even curiosity, mingle with a number of indefinable emotions in the complex psychic state which entertains the thought of God.

Nothing could be more futile than to seek to pattern all thoughts of God, the Soul, and Duty, after one person's conception. Each must fashion his own thought of these truths, and each must respond in his own way to his own God. This does not mean that there are many gods, any more than there are many worlds in which we live. But it does mean that there can be no censor, no Pope or church which can make our thought of God in whom we live.

II

TYPES

THOUGH no two faces are exactly alike, everyone instinctively groups faces into classes. An ability to do this is a valuable asset to a man of affairs; for in many cases the face value of a person is the only value obtainable when a decision is pending. Then the practised eye discerns the alert and the phlegmatic, the vigorous and the incompetent with a remarkable precision. As experience in "character reading" increases, assurance grows. For, in spite of many errors, so many estimates are correct that nearly everyone directs his attitude towards strangers according to the impressions they make. Nor is this a haphazard method. Underlying the diversities of expressions there are general traits which are fairly constant.

Thirty years ago Francis Galton endeavoured to put these vague and popular beliefs into systematic form by making composite photographs of different classes of people. He took several criminals, several persons suffering from consumption, and other cases of physical or mental likeness, and superimposed their pictures. As a result, the features in common stand out with considerable distinctness. Enough similarity is evident to show why one instinctively declares "that is a criminal face," or "that person has tuberculosis." Recently, over a score of photographs of New York bank presidents were thrown into a composite picture. Of course one could not say, " Here is a typical bank president," when looking at the picture. Nevertheless, the intelligence, character and culture of a successful man were all in clear evidence. No one could mistake the lines of that countenance for a pugilist's, or a tramp's, or a debauchee's. Within certain limits, anyone could indicate the social and intellectual status of the man.

As we saw in the preceding chapter, there is a certain correlation between the external form and the internal factors of personality. So, here, we may look for types of human nature as well as types of countenance. Only as such classes appear, can an intelligent study proceed. For it is the first duty of any research to classify. The success in classification measures the grasp of the subject. When Linnæus arranged his plants in the order of their structural similarities, he revolutionized botany; but not until the principles of evolution were understood, did a complete and accurate classification become possible. It is not enough to point out superficial resemblances and to group them as " Types." Some understanding of the forces which enter into the making of types is necessary. For this reason, several chapters will be devoted to the study of a number of elements which go into the forming of the great classes of human beings.

Obviously, the wide *physical* disparity among people will be instrumental in shaping human nature in such a way that one classification will follow those lines. Such characteristic differences as those of sex cannot help dividing the human race into two great types. Some of these characteristic features will be discussed in later chapters. Suffice it, here, to call attention to the evident physical disparity of sex; the skeletal, muscular, organic and functional dissimilarities. So great are these that some writers declare the two sexes can never thoroughly understand each other. They point out how somatic sensations, which furnish a background of affective colouring to all thinking, are so unlike that the two types of mind never hold the same conceptions in the same setting. Less obvious are the physical types in races. Ethnologists show types in shape and capacity of skull, in height and strength of skeleton, colour of hair and eyes. Philologists show types of language which give some insight into the typical workings of the mind. Sociologists point out traits of racial natures arising from conditions of climate, topography and occupation. Historians find unclassifiable particular events, which also mould the spiritual life of races. Each angle of inquiry shows a feature delineating a type. Not all dissimilarities are clear enough to draw clear-cut distinctions, but that is also true in any classification. Enough are clear and distinct to indicate racial types, though the older, classical groupings may be untenable.

National types have less apparent lines of cleavage. Here the changes and chances of history tend to obliterate old societies and create new. Local communities, clans or tribes, are ever assimilating new elements or separating into new groups. The constituencies of a nation are, also, in a state of flux. Nevertheless there are biological and physiological influences which tend to make national types. M. Le Bon declares " the mental constitution of a race is due to very simple physiological reasons. Each individual is the product not merely of his immediate parents but also of his race, that is, of the entire series of his ascendants. A learned economist, M. Cheysson, has calculated that in France, supposing there to be three generations in a century, each of us would have in his veins the blood of at least twenty millions of the people living in the year 1000 A.D. In consequence all the inhabitants of a given locality, of a given district, necessarily possess common ancestors, are moulded of the same clay, bear the same impress, and they are all brought back unceasingly to the average type by this long and heavy chain of which they are merely the last links. We are the children at once of our parents and of our race. . . . The formation of the mental constitution of a people does not demand, as the creation of animal species, those geological periods whose immense duration defies calculation. Still the time it demands is considerable. To create such a people as the French, even to the comparatively slight extent accomplished as yet, the community of sentiments and thought that forms its soul, more than ten centuries have been necessary." *

In Mr. Gehring's fascinating essays upon "Racial Contrasts," some very noteworthy characteristics of the Germanic and Latin peoples are given. These appear very neatly in the musical compositions of the two. A distinguishing trait of Teutonic compositions is their liberal use of counterpoint. "Counterpoint was developed among the Netherlanders, a nation partly Germanic and partly Celtic in their derivation. Two of the great names which mark the evolution of this method of composition, O'Keghern and Willaert, are Germanic. Transplanted to Italy, counterpoint bloomed forth in full splendor in the works of Palestrina; but its barbaric complexity soon led to a reaction among that people of classic tastes, which resulted in the invention of the

* Le Bon: "The Psychology of Peoples," pp. 8, 12.

simpler monadic or harmonic style. Ever since that time, counterpoint has found a more congenial home among the masters of Germanic extraction. Bach was the greatest of all contrapuntists. Händel, Mozart, Beethoven, Wagner and Brahms were all masters of polyphony; the Romanic races, on the contrary, have devoted themselves preferentially to forms of composition which did not admit of florid contrapuntal treatment. . . . The essence of counterpoint is complexity. A single melody is clear and simple in nature; so is a melody with harmonic accompaniment. Although the harmonic basis comprises several tones, these are as a rule not perceived separately, but are incorporated with the melody, clinging to it indissolubly, like colour to a material object. In counterpoint, however, we have two or more independent voices running along side by side with or without harmonic accompaniment. The mind is in a divided state and fluctuates from part to part in the endeavour to hold all the elements together." This extensive diversity of elements which calls for a large grasp of thought is an indication of what psychologists call a broad "span of attention" in those who take pleasure in this class of music. For the attention must needs take hold of many things at once. If it cannot do this, and occupies itself with first one feature of the music and then another, all the symmetry and balance disappear from the composition and the mind receives the impression of a jumble of unrelated passages; which, of course, is displeasing to any musical taste.

Similar principles are to be found in literature. The Germanic abounds in figurative expressions which open out vistas to the imagination, they are so full of suggestions. Germanic style is prolific with detail. The drama swarms with a multitude of persons, scenes, interests; witness Goethe's "Faust." Latin people prefer clearness. "Germanic sentences with their extreme length, employment of auxiliary words, suspension of sense and crowding of intermediate parts with modifying adjectives, participles and dependent clauses," require a broad-spanned attention to keep all the factors of the thought present to the mind. Not only is a broad grasp of the attention needed, but a certain agility of mind; for the intelligibility of each sentence depends upon the ability to recall quickly and accurately the significance of each word. This seems to be a characteristic of the Teutonic mind.

In German art, too, there was the peculiar crowding of compositions, and the multiplied and angular folds of the drapery, while not elegant, tended to increase the points of attention. Italian artists stripped their pictures of accessions. Many of the most famous among them, as a rule, introduced but a limited number of figures. Giotto, Bellini, Raphael and Titian are examples. Michael Angelo criticised the Northern custom of painting "landscapes," with "many figures scattered here and there." Rubens, on the other hand, delighted in a bewildering profusion of elements. "The figures in northern art, as a rule, embody more individuality; they are more heterogeneous, while those in the South tend to homogeneity. There is much sameness in the faces and poses of the southern paintings. As a result, the mind is not engaged in so many directions; a group of people can often be perceived as a single object,—a mere group; the battalions of Meissonier, for example, 'sing' in unison; in the North, on the contrary, the constituent figures demand more attention."

Mr. Gehring's study shows how a few salient mental and temperamental traits, identified with a people, will shine out in their works. Everyone recognizes the profundity of Germanic thought and the lucidity of Latin expression; but not many recognize the deep-seated psychological facts which give rise to these often noticed characteristics. Here, however, the trail-marks appear so clear that one may easily trace the influence of a mental endowment which differentiates two great European peoples. For the common characteristics, in the several means which are considered, of expressing the mental life can be due to but one class of ability; namely, that of attention. By which is meant the ability to hold in the "clearness area" of consciousness a number of impressions at a given time. Thus, one man catches the entire display in a shop window with a glance where another sees only a few details. A difference in span of attention accounts for this simple experience. On a larger scale, the same thing applies to the faculty of grasping an involved passage in music, an intricate sentence in reading, a large grouping of forms, or colours, in statuary, or painting. Much more will be said on this head in another place, but it must be added here that attention is the "clearest area" of consciousness, something as the circle of light about a torch gradually dims into complete darkness. In the semi-light of attention many things are dimly apprehended. Vague impressions of the glass on the shop window, the colour of the sill, the curtain in the background, may stay in this "fringe" of the attention. When the attention is of the narrow-spanned type there will be little in this field. All that is clearly seen or heard will apparently be all that exists at the time. So a musical theme, or a problem in philosophy, will have many or few tributary impressions as the mind apprehends through a broad-spanned attention with a wide margin, or fringe, or through a narrow-spanned attention with no surrounding and faint perceptions. Needless to say, the religious outlook upon the universe will be very different in these two types of mind.

Another great cause of typical resemblances is in the family. The same heredity and home influence produce many noticeable resemblances among individuals. From generation to generation the same germ plasm carries the possibility of similar development. Mendel proved for the vegetal world that a proportion of the traits of either parent were handed down unalloyed to their descendants, and, in some measure, the principle appears among human beings. Darwin and Galton showed many instances of very important resemblances between parent and progeny. However, such resemblances are from groups too small to be of any considerable influence upon the social order, and do not materially affect the religious type.

Beyond these Types, which are assigned to those agencies which form races and families, are many Types whose character is determined by less easily recognized causes. For example, there is a criminal type, which is the result of psychological weakness plus sociological injustice; there is an artistic type, which springs from a high development of certain faculties and a coöperative appreciation from society. Then there are the Tramp, the Scholar, the Inventor, the Adventurer, the Mechanic and a host of others. All owe their kind to a combination of social and physiological causes. The psychological causes are, in a measure, identical with those which enter into the making of genus and species the world over. The social causes are of a very subtile but equally effective kind. M. Tarde has explained at great length that human conduct follows the laws of Imitation in the same way that the animal kingdom repeats its species according to the laws of heredity, or as the vibration in physics reproduces itself in succeeding vibrations. Whatever may be said of the philosophy of this theory, it is undoubtedly true that a great number of our activities, our pleasures and our beliefs are the result of imitation. Professor Giddings finds the cause of grouping among all conscious creatures in the "consciousness of kind." Birds of a feather, and men of like tastes, flock together. Here is a clear and forceful reason for the formation and maintenance of typical groups of men. Everyone appreciates the influence of the same sort of occupation to produce fraternity of feeling and unity of outlook. The same kinds of traditions which give direction to ideas and purposes are potent in creating types of mind. Many other great influences, (which call for the same reactions among a large number of people, such as laws, customs, morals), have a great formative effect upon human nature and leave their unmistakable imprint. If the results of these influences are compared, it will become evident that the forces of nature and society are constantly gathering the innumerable individualities of humanity into characteristic Types.

In general, there are two great classes of influences acting to produce types of men. One is physical, the other is social. The former gives an inherent disposition toward the same sort of thinking, feeling and acting among people sharing the same heritage. It is not by chance, then, that women respond to the appeal of religion in the Christian churches and Buddhist temples more than men; nor is it strange that the people of the north of Europe, whose art, literature and philosophy show such a contrast with their Southern neighbours, should become Protestant so much more easily. The latter, the social influences, give customs, morals and habits to the groups of people upon whom they act. These result in typical traits which are often easily recognized. The people, for example, in the conservative sections of the country where the influences of a former generation still live, still think and feel upon political and religious matters in a characteristic way.

We may conclude, therefore, that each mind has its own life which, in detail, is unlike any other, but which, in its general cast, may be classed with many others. Nature and society conspire to create original individuals, and both physical nature and the social order conspire to give these individualities characteristic uniformities. These different natures show their individuality in the conception of religious truth, and where genuine types of religious nature are found, there appear types of religious experience and beliefs.

III

RELIGIONS AND RELIGION

FROM the preceding chapters we are prepared to find a variety of religions passing under the one name, Religion. Each individual works out his *own* salvation. It is his, and his alone, though he shares its elements with a host of his fellows. As a bed of flowers draws its life from one blazing star, millions of miles distant, each plant receiving the same light, but each sending out its leaves to receive the light in its own way; so, in the hosts of human lives, each grows in its own way under the one Light. There is no need in this inquiry to study that Light, " which lighteth every man that cometh into the world," any more than the botanist, seeking to find the cause of the differences in the growth of his plants, needs to study the sun. If the warmth of sunshine is constant, shining upon each equally, it cannot be the cause of differences. These must be due to diverse and varying causes which act unequally upon plant or human nature. The present study is in psychology, not in theology. Our interest is in types of religious life and the factors which cause these types. If the Infinite Being is Father of all men, and makes His sun to shine on the just and the unjust, then the differences in religious life have a human origin, and are to be studied by psychology. If there is no God and the religious life is spontaneously engendered, then, obviously, it is to be studied by psychology. Whether the theist or the atheist is right, religious differences find their origin in *human nature!*

Individuality and types of human nature give birth to individual differences and types in the religious life. Professor James B. Pratt * has sought to find the bases of religious belief by having a number of people describe their religious life in response to a *questionnaire*. This *questionnaire* contains the following questions: First, what does religion mean to you personally? That is, is it a belief that something exists? Is it an emotional experience, is it an attitude of the will toward God or toward righteousness, or is it something else? Second, what do you mean by God? Third, why do you believe in God? Fourth, do you not so much believe in God as to want to use Him? Fifth, is God very real to you; as real as an earthly friend, though different? Sixth, do you pray, and if so, why? Seventh, what do you mean by spirituality? Eighth, do you believe in personal immortality? Ninth, do you accept the Bible as authority in religious matters? Tenth, what do you mean by a religious experience? These questions were answered by two classes of people: the one was what Professor Pratt called "typical church people," the other he describes as a "somewhat motley collection of intellectual people." In all there were sixty-eight replies. Among these sixty-eight people we find great differences in the religious life. Perhaps individuality shows in no other one department of life quite so clearly as it does in the religious experience. Professor Pratt finds these many diverse religious principles falling into five classes. The first class contains those whose reli-

* *Amer. Jour. of Relig. Psychol., 2,* pp. 76-96.

gious life builds up upon intellectual factors. That is, the reason furnishes the basis of religion. Such people can give a reason for the faith that is in them. They can supply you arguments why they believe as they do and why they live as they do. Said one, "I believe in God as an intellectual and moral necessity. Any feelings which I may have in the matter grow out of the perception of the realities which cause these necessities —God is a reality to me as a rational being." Said another, "I believe in God because I cannot conceive of a world like ours except as made and controlled by a person."

The second class comprises those who believe in God because they have been so instructed and their instruction has been urged upon them by those whom they consider authoritative. In such a class would fall the great majority of those who find the Church the keystone of their faith and those who find the Bible the cornerstone of their belief. As one Roman Catholic remarked, "If I want to know about God I go to the Church as represented by some priest, for the Church is the authority in religious matters, just as the physician and teacher are in their sphere." Of course, there are multitudes of Protestants who would answer as one respondent did, "I believe in God from authority, as contained in the Bible in passages declaring themselves as God, as, 'I am God and there is none else; I am God and there is none like Me.' There are many other assurances that might be quoted."

There are not so many church people who hold to the Bible's authority as is often supposed. Of the forty-four answers from church people, thirty accepted and fourteen rejected the Book's authority, twenty-two saying that their religious faith and religious life were based on it. That is, exactly half of the typical religious people who answered the questions feel that their belief and their religion are dependent on the old way of viewing the Bible, the other half feeling independent for their religious life from its authority or rejecting it (in the old sense) altogether.

The third class is made up of those who are religious because they have started in the religious life and have continued in its momentum, finding it easier to continue than to desert. This sounds cynical, but it is not. For our lives are made up of many tendencies which have become woven together, and to which we adhere unreasonably. Here is a typical answer. " Entirely a matter of training. I was brought up in the Presbyterian Church—took pride in being an Atheist all through my college course—though always attended church and Sunday-school." Another curious answer is, " My religion is a bundle of inconsistencies which I have long ago quit trying to reconcile."

The fourth class contains those whose belief grows out of need. They believe in God and live in the strength of that belief because they find life is bettered and brightened by such a course. Said one, " Because I personally, subjectively want to believe in Him. I pray because I like to. I believe in immortality because I like to." Said another, after several years of scepticism and argument he came back " to the plain solid ideas which were drilled into us in childhood. Then comes a peace of mind regarding our religious status." It is from this class that the Christian church has always found a champion to defend the old, the established, and sometimes the absurd.

The fifth class is characterized by that most prevalent factor in religion, *feeling*. Dr. Pratt found that thirty-six out of his sixty-eight respondents belong in this class and fourteen of the remaining claimed, also, to have had some mystical experience. That is, fifty people out of sixty-eight firmly believed that they had been in immediate communion with God. This belief was based upon experience. The following are typical responses. " His presence I find in the deeps of Nature and of human nature. I never feel so devotional as when in a great wood where I cannot see out, on the sea, on the seashore, or out at night under the stars." " In one sense He is real; when I see the sunlight shining through the leaves or the forest trees and lighting up the ferns and flowers unseen by anyone else save myself, I have felt a nearness of God that I have never felt under the influence of any sermon." "God as my Father is very real. Have I experienced His presence? Yes, and more than once." "I do feel that I have experienced His presence very distinctly many times." " I came to Him a dying drunkard and He gave me repentance. I cried to Him and He saved me instantly. I have never wanted a drink, nor sworn an oath, nor stolen a cent since."

We cannot draw very many deductions from the experiences of sixty-eight people; but one deduction we surely can draw and that is, there are wide diversities in the religious lives of different people. The question suggests itself,—are these answers accurately descriptive of their author's religion? Every psychologist knows how difficult it is to " introspect." Indeed, it requires an exceptional talent to look into one's life and describe one's thoughts or feelings accurately. It is a very nice question whether such a performance can be accomplished at all or not. Certainly a miscellaneous group of people could not give us very *definite* descriptions of the most subtle experiences. Their answers are valuable. They are studies from real life. They are snapshots of portions of actual life. They certainly make clear the diversity in religion due to individuality and the rough resemblances between them are strongly indicative of types.

Let us supplement these statements by a study of the careful statements of specialists in the field of religious thought. Professor Leuba has gathered a number of definitions of religion, which come from the facile pens of several of our religious philosophers.* Here, too, we find a most bewildering diversity of opinions in which it is hard to find two definitions alike. Professor Leuba groups them: "On examining the definitions of religion, one finds that a psychological classification in three groups makes room for them all. Several other classifications are possible. We give the preference to the following because it brings into relief better than any other the faulty psychology which enters for so large a share in this lamentable confusion of ideas about religion. In the first, a specific intellectual element is given, as the essence or as the distinguishing mark of religion. In the second, it is one of several objective feelings singled out as the religious differentia; while in the third group, the active principle, the cravings, the desires, the impulses, the will, take the place occupied by the intellect or the feelings in the other classes. Religion becomes, in this view, an endeavour to realize a certain type of being, an instinct, a certain kind of

* *Monist, II*, pp. 195-225.

actions, etc." In the first group of definitions, in which the intellectual element dominates, we have Martineau, who defines religion as, "A belief in an ever-living God, that is, in a divine mind and will ruling the universe, and holding moral relations with mankind." Romanes' definition is, "Religion is a department of thought having for its objects superconsciousness and intelligent being." D'Alviella thought that "The belief in the existence of superhuman beings, who interfere in a mysterious fashion in the destiny of man, constitutes religion."

The second group of definitions contains those actuated by feeling. Schleiermacher declared, "Religion cannot and will not originate in the pure impulse to know. It is neither thinking nor acting, but intuition and feeling." Herbart wrote, "Sympathy with the universal dependence of men is the essential natural principle of all religion." Daniel G. Thompson thought, "Religion is the aggregate of those sentiments in the human mind arising in connection with the relations assumed to subsist between the order of nature and a postulated supernatural."

In the third group we find the following definitions. Bradley declared, "Religion is the attempt to express the complete reality of goodness through every aspect of our being." Another definition is that of Feuerbach, "The origin, nay, the essence of religion is desire; if a man possess no needs, no desires, he would possess no good." Marshall said, "The restraint of individualistic impulses to rational ones (the suppression of our will to a higher will) seems to me to be of the very essence of religion; the belief in the Deity, as usually found, is, from the psychological point of view, an attachment to, rather than the essence of, the religious feeling."

It would appear from these groups of definitions, that the trained thinker finds as great a difficulty in agreeing with his neighbour's religious conceptions as does the average man. Perhaps the only difference is that the religious philosopher endeavours to universalize what he finds in his own religious experience. He judges others by himself. While the man on the street would simply look within and try to state what his own personal religious life is. There is this agreement between them both, the philosopher and the average man may be classed in one of three groups. He will find his group in accordance with the dominance of some one element in his religious nature; whether it be reason, or emotion, or the disposition for action.

Some very interesting efforts have been made to find a unity in all religions by tracing back their history toward their origins. This is a thoroughly orthodox scientific proceeding. It is the comparative method. It has yielded magnificent results. Time was, not so many years ago, when the diversity of languages was a bewildering puzzle. Comparative philology succeeded in tracing back the numerous dialects to their paternal languages and these parental languages back to one remote tongue; in the case of the Aryan languages. The Semitic languages seem to have a family tree of their own. In comparative anatomy and embryology, the relationship of the whole animal kingdom promises to be disclosed. From these striking precedents we are surely authorized to hope for great results when the comparative method seeks, in the evolution of religions, the remote parental religion. At present, however, the theories concerning the origin of religion are not very convincing. A generation ago Herbert Spencer sought to convince the thinking world that religion took its origin amid the superstitions of primitive man. When the primitive man heard a voice resound from a mountain-side in response to his own cry, he knew nothing of the echo and so interpreted the reply as from an unseen speaker. When he dreamt at night, he thought the visions he saw were as real as the objects he beheld in the daylight. The face which looked up into his from the smooth waters of the spring was no human face; but it, too, could only be explained as the echo, and as the vision of the dead in his dream, by an appeal to the supernatural. If we grant that the superstitions of primitive man originated in this way, which seems probable, we are still a very long distance from explaining the religious nature of man. For these interpretations would not be wrought into the fibre of human nature. Their influence would disappear as science appeared. Among highly educated families to-day, where these superstitions play no part in their religious development, there is a heart-hunger which seeks satisfaction. In many cases, such a satisfaction is found quite independently of that body of ideas which relate to the phenomena Mr. Spencer described. A much more serious effort to explain the origin of the religious nature has been undertaken by McDougall.* His endeavour is to trace out the beginnings of the emotions rather than the ideas which underlie religion. He believes that the emotions which play a principal part in the religious life are admiration, awe and reverence. He seeks to show how these emotions originated in our ancestors. The primitive man lacked almost completely the con-

*Wm. McDougall: "An Introduction to Social Psychology," Chapter XIII.

ception of mechanical causation. When bodies fell to the ground, when the wind blew, when the sun rose, when the lightning flashed and the thunder crashed, when the rain fell and extinguished the fire, all these phenomena had to be explained in some way. The one kind of causation with which he was familiar was his own voluntary action issuing from feeling, emotion and desire. So this naturally became the type upon which he modelled his theories of causation. The pestilence, famine, storm, disease and flood which worked such dreadful havoc must surely be caused by some sinister being. Naturally, he stood in awe of such a being or beings. " As soon as these powers began to be conceived by man as personal powers, they must have evoked in him the attitude and impulse of subjection and the emotion of negative self-feeling, which are rooted in the instinct of subjection. . . . He not only feared and wondered at these powers but humbled himself before them, and sought to gain and to obey the slightest indication of their wills." This attitude gave rise to customs which sought to placate the unseen powers. As time passed, these customs would take on an ever-increasing strong hold upon man, they would have the sanctity and authority of antiquity, and they would be perpetuated as the people's most priceless heritage. As men rose to higher stages of culture, the fearsome aspects of their faith would give place to a better understanding of Nature, and into their religion tenderer emotions would find their way." This change in the nature of the religious emotions among those peoples that have survived and progressed was a natural consequence of their success in the struggle of groups for survival. For the surviving communities are those whose gods have, in the main, not only spared them, not only abstained from bringing plague and famine and military disaster upon them in too severe measures, but have actually supported them and helped them to overcome their enemies." In some such way as this, gratitude would enter into the religious emotion. Later, as social life became more complex, and ideas of justice arose, the community would elevate its god, and imputing higher attributes to it, the religious life would correspondingly rise. The criticism of this theory which instantly occurs to mind is this: it takes emotions already developed and groups them into an instinct. These emotions may become part of one's being and become transmitted to posterity, but a combination of such emotions could hardly be transmitted. Furthermore, when we look into the origin of the religious life in the individual, we do not always find the emotions McDougall mentions. I think of a case, with which I am very familiar, in which the religious life took its inception in a passionate love of the Divine Being. I cannot find that fear of any sort played any part in the upspringing of a religion which practically made a new character in this young man. Then, too, if we can rely upon the "theory of recapitulation," to understand the early life-history of the race, there must have been something in the race-history to correspond with the adolescent period. McDougall's theories might well be ascribed to a sort of pre-adolescent race-history. The storm and stress of the formative period of the race, in which our modern religious life probably had its origin, is not described in the experience of primitive man.

Perhaps it should be said in passing that the theories advanced to explain the appearance of religion among men have nothing whatever to do with the validity of religion itself. In the minds of many people, any explanation of the forces which might have operated in the past of the race to induce religious thinking and feeling is more than an explanation. It is a destructive calamity. Surely this is absurd. One might as well claim that there could be no philosophy, no understanding of the universe because the brain of man may be traced back to the ganglia of the protozoa. In view of the fact that we know so little about the relation of brain to mind, it is most ridiculous to set limits to philosophic truths in terms of nerve-history. There may well be communion between the finite spirit and the Infinite Spirit brought about in some of the astonishing processes in the evolution of man. When we recall that we draw our breath by means of an organ which in the remote past served as an air bladder for water animals, it is not incredible that the means by which we have our spiritual life should have served in the remote past some other and very different purpose.

Whether religion has its spirit from natural and social forces, or comes from Spirit to spirit, it matters not. It is the supreme value in human life. Its value is not to be found in the Past, but in its worth at this hour. We are not antiquarians. We are living souls!

The question in hand is briefly this, shall we speak of Religions or of Religion? Despite the diversity and the testimonies of the average man, despite the diversities of definitions of the religious philosopher, there is a widespread conviction that some people are religious and some are not religious, and that the religious people are characterized by something they have in common. That is, the word religion conveys a fairly definite general idea. The confusion in which we find ourselves when we try to define religion in terms of someone's religion, is a confusion which appears whenever we attempt to understand the general through the particular. Throughout the world men are engaged in earning a livelihood. What a task it would be to explain what work is! Such an explanation would have to include a South Sea islander shaking nuts off of a tree and Madame Curie making polonium. The panorama of all human beings doing millions of different things promises ill for a definition of work. There is, however, this in common to them all; they are all urged on by the desire to live. This desire for well-being expresses itself in a myriad of ways. In much the same way, there is a desire for well-being among religious people. They seek this well-being in a host of different ways. The point is, that they seek it. It is not hard to distinguish between the worker and the non-worker, and it is not hard to distinguish between the religious and the non-religious. It is not necessary to use a clear definition of religion. It is sufficient to remember that the religious man finds life incomplete and he seeks to round it out. He deliberates and represents to his mind certain "systems of truths," and these make his world a more intelligible and inhabitable world. His heart hungers for a happiness which he cannot find apart from what he terms his communion with God; he is prompted to many courses of action which he would not take were he not actuated by a desire for spiritual enlargement. So the only unity we may find in religion is a unity of motive. This we do find, whether it is in the Indian beseeching his gods to give him skill in the chase that he may enjoy life and prestige among his fellows, or whether it is a Gladstone seeking in the quiet of Westminster Abbey strength for the guidance of an empire. The motive is the desire for a more efficient Self as each one understands efficiency and himself.

Of course, there is a unity in the Christian religion which is based upon its historical past. All Christianity employs practically the same body of writings, and in large divisions of the Church there is a unity due to tradition; tradition not only of interpretation but of thought, feeling and custom. Imitation plays a large part in levelling down natural differences. Indeed, some of the subtle spiritual experiences of the Christian, which often characterize a large number of worshippers, are due to an imitation of each other, unconscious but effective. Nevertheless, despite the same sources of instruction,—the Scriptures, the Church, the customs of the past,—there are innumerable differences to be found among those holding the Christian faith, these differences being based upon individuality which no levelling force externally imposed can obliterate. We shall find that these differences may also be grouped into types.

IV

THE SECTS

IT is a very common opinion that the religious life in the United States is declining. There seem to be so many indications of this that it is rather rare to find anyone maintaining the opposite view. The many idle churches, the rows of vacant pews are constantly pointed to as arguments that the Church is losing its hold upon the masses of the people. More pertinent to the close observer is the lack of vigour which characterizes religion. Pessimism within the Church, criticism of the Church, a widespread conviction that something is wrong with organized Christianity characterize the situation to-day. In innumerable ways this dissatisfaction expresses itself. One of the "Six Best Sellers" contrasts the life of to-day with antebellum days. The narrative turns upon the sharp contrast between the customs, ideas and ideals of our forefathers and our own. One striking fact is strongly emphasized; in the language of the author we have "ceased to be a religious people." Such a sentiment goes unchallenged. It is simply accepted as one of the obvious things which everybody nowadays is familiar with.

Against this general consensus of opinion, the government "Report upon Religious Bodies in the United States for the Year 1906" urges a tremendous argument. In the long columns of close-written figures an astonishing eulogy of the Church is wrought out. It appears that over thirty-two million people in the United States are communicants in the Christian churches. Compared with the population of 1906, there were 391 church members for every 1,000 people. In 1850 there were only 149 church members for every 1,000 persons. That is, the proportion of church members to the whole population has much more than doubled. This is a strange way for organized religion to die! In the last sixteen years the nation has been growing very rapidly; but the church membership has been growing more rapidly. In 1890, 32.7 per cent. of the population belonged to the Church. In 1906, 39.1 per cent. of the people were enrolled in the churches. Of course, much of this great growth is due to immigration from Roman Catholic countries; but when that is deducted, we still have the significant fact that the Protestant membership in the churches increased from 22.3 per cent. in 1890 to 24.1 per cent. in 1906.

These figures do not tell the whole story, for we must remember that a large portion of the population is ineligible to church membership; there are millions of children who by the rules of many churches cannot be members. Moreover, there are thousands of adherents to the churches who are not communicants. In many cases these people are faithful supporters of the churches and are frequently among its most devout subscribers.

Another impressive feature in this great census argument appears in the figures representing the wealth of the Church. Over a billion, two hundred-fifty millions of dollars are invested in church property. What a

THE SECTS

tremendous power is represented there! Another indication of the colossal power of the Church is this: in one year over thirty-eight millions of dollars were applied to Christian purposes, over twelve millions went into the spreading of Christian ideals and the Christian life in missions at home, over seventeen millions were spent in educating the youth of the land, while eight millions more went into hospitals and asylums. Another fund of over eight millions crossed the seas to spread the spirit of Christ in foreign lands.

Had we only the statement of the census and no other data for our judgment, we should conclude that the Christian church of the United States was the most powerful organization in the world. With its colossal aggregation of people who have pledged themselves to follow Christ; with the immense wealth invested in their plants and the great sums continually applied in furthering their cause, surely, their influence should be irresistible. When we recall the effective work done by much smaller bodies, with much smaller resources, in every period of history, it would be but natural to expect the very greatest achievements from American Christianity. Why is it, then, that the Church is so ineffective? Why is it that throughout the land there is a unanimous conviction that the Church is almost a negligible factor in national life? Scores of smaller organizations with very much less wealth make themselves much more effectively felt. In the great moral issues, in the great ethical crises, this tremendous body of people seems supine and inert.

The evidence of the Church's weakness appears also in the census, wrapped up with the evidences of its strength. This great body is not a unit. It is a composition of many factions. Instead of one great Church, it is one hundred eighty-six denominations. Surely it is a wonder that a house so divided stands at all. Nor does the spirit of the times seem to affect its disposition to divide against itself. For in 1890 there were 145 denominations, and in 1906 there were 41 more. Not all of these, however, were brought into existence by schisms, though seventeen had their origin in the spirit of secession. If the denominations were arranged alphabetically in great families, we should find almost every one a victim of this unchristian malady. The Adventists head the list, a comparatively young denominational family. It is split into seven branches. (There are the Evangelical Adventists, the Life and Advent Union, the Advent Christian Church, Seventh Day Adventists, Church of God, Churches of God, Churches of God in Jesus Christ.) The next great family, the Baptist, falls into sixteen divisions. The next denominational body, the "Brethren," contains a little over ten thousand people. These Brethren display their brotherly spirit by splitting into four branches. There are the "Exclusives," the Open Brethren, a sort of a high-church branch, and a fourth division which issued from this last in 1890. And so the denominational history goes. It is too long and too monotonous to follow through alphabetically. The five largest Protestant families are these: the Methodists with fifteen divisions, the Baptists with sixteen, the Presbyterians with twelve, the Lutherans with twenty-four, the Disciples of Christ with only two. The Disciples are one of the strongest and most rapidly growing churches in the country. Their comparative unity indicates the possibility of unity among others. And it offers a strong argument against the devastating spirit of the sects.

The outcome of these many divisions should have been foreseen generations ago. There is a seating capacity of over fifty-eight millions in the church buildings of these 186 sects; that is, there is room enough for nearly twice their number of members. A large portion of that billion dollars is invested in empty seats. In the language of the Trusts, " The plants in this organization have been ruinously duplicated." This overlapping of church organization is a most obvious source of weakness, though a number of the sects take a pride in multiplying their plants. Indeed, some Home Mission Boards consider their effectiveness only in terms of new churches started. If the poor and puny lives of these little churches flicker and then go out, their demise is not attributed to a difficulty in church strategy, but rather to a lack of the Holy Spirit in the work of the little organization so foolishly started. Such sectarian zeal is well enough in many instances. It quickly puts a church of some kind into a new community, and that is valuable service. However, when a country is well settled, then a new church may be an evil. It may violate the law of demand and supply. The missionary society that forces a church upon a community which is already well churched, does so in the expectation that a demand for this church will appear later. In very many cases no such demand ever arises, and so such superfluous churches are not only a loss to the Christian cause but an obstruction to the work of the other churches. Though this evil is very widely spread throughout the country, it is not felt so keenly in the large cities as in the smaller towns; for in the large cities there is more apt to be a greater field for the individual church; though in downtown districts, where the church-going population has thinned out, this competition is often a serious matter.

The following facts of church life—or perhaps we should say church strife—in two little towns of the West are very characteristic. In one town of 800 souls * in a far western state there are eight church organizations, Roman Catholic, Presbyterian, Baptist, three Lutheran, and two Methodist. There are five church buildings, all of them ugly, unpainted, ill-kept, poorly furnished. These inhospitable eyesores have been struggling for years to maintain themselves. Not one is able to support a minister without generous donations from its parent denomination. The presence of the Catholic church is understood. The three Lutheran churches are divided along racial lines, German, Scandinavian and Danish. The two Methodist churches represent the Northern and Southern divisions. They are " located on opposite corners of the same block, with nothing between them, the building of the latter enjoys the preeminence of being higher up on the hillside; but this advantage is offset to some extent by the greater size of the former's steeple." Organized Christianity in this little town has one Catholic and seven Protestant bodies. There is a constant succession of ministers who undertake to improve the moral and religious condition of the town and who give up in despair. There are long periods during which a pulpit will be vacant and the Sunday-school will try to keep up the church life. The services of the churches are very poorly attended and dispiriting, the best singers being scattered among the

* Wm. Boyle: "Transplanted Denominationalism," *The Outlook, 83,* p. 323.

different churches. "An un-Christian spirit of envy and jealousy is aroused by the temporary success of any one of the churches." This large number of churches in so small a place does not augur a high moral standard or widespread religious habits. For three or four months in summer all the stores are kept open on Sunday. Four saloons do business seven days in the week, with their accompaniments of gambling and lewdness. When low shows visit the town they are very well attended. "The sensuous and the pleasure-loving spirit is everywhere in evidence." Mr. Boyle believes that "denominationalism is directly responsible for these conditions. Too weak to assert any influence alone, and too jealous to act together, the churches do not command the respect of the community, and are unable to stand the tide of prevailing evil. Each minister is too timid to oppose the prevalent evil customs alone, dreading the reflex action of possible sentiment on himself and his feeble church. . . . Strange to say, the denominational spirit of the town is not strong. Whenever there are special attractions at any one church in the way of music or of a strange preacher, members of other churches do not hesitate to flock there, leaving their own minister to preach to empty pews. The Presbyterian church has on its roll the names of men and women who have been connected with ten different denominations elsewhere, several of which are represented here. Certainly in this case it is neither doctrines nor form of government that brings them together. Members of one church frequently transfer their membership to another church, for reasons having no connection with doctrines or polity. A large majority of the members would be unable to give an intelligent account of the distinctive differences in the belief of the different denominations."

Another interesting study of a small town in the West reveals a similar situation.* Another little Western town of 1,347 inhabitants has eight different denominations and seven church buildings, two of which are unused, and the third open only two or three times a year. Each of the English-speaking Evangelical churches hopes that the other will die and end the bitter competition. The feeble efforts for consolidation have failed, because of a few radical sectarians and the zeal of the mission secretaries. The population of the little city shows by the state census of 1905 that 65 per cent. of the people are born of foreign parentage, so only 475 are of American descent now. Studies in church attendance show that some 15 per cent. to 50 per cent. of the population is church-going. "Taking five as a normal family the number of possible English-speaking Evangelical church-goers in X is about 285; admitting that 50 per cent. of them attend church regularly we have 142 constant attendants. (This figure is above the real attendance.) Again using our average family we get 95 per cent. heads of households, 45 of which will admit as subscribers for church support. A church which raises $1,500 a year for all purposes is perhaps on a normal and possible basis; such a church needs 50 subscribers and an average subscription of $30 (which is again higher than the average for small towns). *A priori*—the town is capable of supporting one live, self-respecting religious organization for its American population. The seating capacity of the English-speaking churches is 825, nearly double the American population.

* A. J. Kennedy: "Religious Living," *Independent, 64,* p. 795.

The church buildings cost $21,300; $7,400 lies absolutely idle and worthless. The inner history of these forlorn churches is rather painful reading. A Congregational church was established in 1871. It has been assisted by the missionary society, and in 1906 the society had paid $10,504 for its support. A Methodist church appeared on the scene in 1873 and continued its work until 1902, receiving $3,700 aid. A Baptist church crowded into this little community in 1879, and in 1906 had received $3,100 aid. In 1882 an Episcopal church endeavoured to establish itself, but gave up the struggle in 1891. In all, these struggling little churches received $18,154 from their parent churches to carry on their ineffectual and demoralizing competition.

"Such a condition as that outlined above brings religion into discredit in the community; causes many to scoff at the Church; takes the heart out of zealous lay workers; and makes it difficult for a minister of religion to hold up his head. . . . The writer has been told of one missionary secretary who boasted before his denominational convention that while he had never disobeyed the rule of his church, which makes it necessary to have three persons to constitute the local church, he had organized many a church with one lay person, himself and God. It is unnecessary to add that this denomination is notorious for the number of its dead churches." There is a crying need for some interdenominational union work to decide what denomination should enter into a new field. There is also a great need for a union of missionary societies to weed out dead churches.

The evils of over-churching a community are perpetuated. No church willingly gives up its career, for this often means a loss of employment, a possible loss of property and almost inevitably a sacrifice of pride. When a church has struggled for years to maintain itself, it usually engenders a spirit of antagonism toward other churches. This antagonism frequently runs out into social cliques. So intense is the feeling in many cases that members of one church will not attend the services of another church should the missionary societies close their own church doors. However, such spirit is so thoroughly anti-Christian that it would seem to make little difference whether people of that ilk had a church to worship in or not. Certainly it is a duty of those who have any control of the situation to starve many of these hostile little organizations into decency. The evil, of course, does not cease in the mere overlapping of churches, in their own localities, but reaches back to the mother-heart of the parent church, where an appeal is constantly made for the means of spreading the gospel, and often the appeal is met with great generosity and noble sacrifices, in the misleading illusion that the money will be spent in spreading the principles of Christianity. If the real situation were presented to the people who help sustain these innumerable conflicting churches, a remedy would not be far to seek. Perhaps the subtle evils are the worst. Diversion of attention from the central purposes of Christianity to the necessities of organization, can only mean a subversion of great ideals. The tone and the temper of the work are vitiated. It is, also, a great loss to be deprived of the inspiration of fellowship in a great work, or a great movement. But it is an incomparably greater loss and far more dispiriting to champion the petty interests of a conflicting denomination. The inspiration alone

THE SECTS

which would arise from a genuine coöperation of all the American churches would in itself far outweigh any particular sacrifices which might be occasioned.

The welfare of American Christianity is a matter of acute interest to every intelligent citizen. The Church is one of many social institutions which go into the making of that form of society we call civilized. It is an institution for which no substitute has been found. Its many avenues of help to the afflicted, or needy, are like the irrigating canals of a dry land; when the reservoirs are full of water, fruits and flowers spring up all along the lines of the canals. When the water system is in disorder, meagre crops and withered vegetation are in evidence everywhere. The result of putting the church system in order would show immediately in many ways. Dispirited and hopeless little churches would give place to efficient and successful churches. Colleges crying for aid to keep up a denominational name would give their vigour to fewer institutions, but to more students. Hospitals would feel the boon of the savings (from the sectarian battles) which would minister to the sick. Men who have prayed in foreign lands for dollars, where dollars mean the new civilization, would have the desire of their lives answered. There is a "third party" in the warfare of the sects, *the public*. It has its rights in this conflict as truly as in the conflicts of capital and labour. The public cannot be ignored. It will take the situation in its own hands, if the leaders in the Church cannot lead the way out of the present chaos. The unconscious drifting from the old attitude of respect and reverence toward the Church will become a conscious and determined revolt against an aggregation of self-centred sects. Then some substitute will be tried, perhaps found, which will make for unity in well-doing, if not in thinking. This the various orders of fraternal societies have almost succeeded in doing. A few more great movements of a similar character, and the Church as an organization will be too pitifully crippled to do the work expected of it.

The 186 sects are an anachronism, and are out of keeping with the spirit of the American people. The very recital of the list of sects, as seen below, is an indictment of them and an aspersion upon their loyalty to the real spirit of Christianity. It tells a story of real danger to which both the patriot and the Christian must hearken. For it is impossible that the multitude of little sects shall continue to multiply, or, indeed, to continue to retain their separate organizations. The first step, of course, is for each denominational family to put its house in order. This would be a great step in advance, for there are many divisions in denominational families throughout the list.

The various sects are arranged below in the order of the last Religious Census.

Denomination	*Number of Members*
ALL DENOMINATIONS	32,936,445
PROTESTANT BODIES	20,287,742
ADVENTIST BODIES	92,735
Advent Christian Church	26,799
Seventh-day Adventist Denomination	62,211
Other Adventists (5 bodies)	3,725
BAPTIST BODIES	5,662,234
Baptists	5,323,183
Northern Baptist Convention	1,052,105
Southern Baptist Convention	2,009,471
National Baptist Convention (Coloured)	2,261,607
Free Baptists	81,359
Freewill Baptists	40,280
General Baptists	30,097

THE SECTS

Denomination	Number of Members
Primitive Baptists	102,311
Coloured Primitive Baptists in America	35,076
Other Baptists (8 bodies)	49,928
CHRISTIANS (Christian Connection)	110,117
CHURCH OF CHRIST, SCIENTIST	85,717
CONGREGATIONALISTS	700,480
DISCIPLES OR CHRISTIANS	1,142,359
Disciples of Christ	982,701
Churches of Christ	159,658
DUNKERS OR GERMAN BAPTIST BRETHREN	97,144
German Baptist Brethren Church (Conservative)	76,547
Other Dunkers (3 bodies)	20,597
EVANGELICAL BODIES	174,780
Evangelical Association	104,898
United Evangelical Church	69,882
FRIENDS	113,172
Society of Friends (Orthodox)	91,161
Other Friends (3 bodies)	22,611
GERMAN EVANGELICAL PROTESTANT BODIES	34,704
GERMAN EVANGELICAL SYNOD OF NORTH AMERICA	293,137
INDEPENDENT CHURCHES	73,673
LUTHERAN BODIES	2,112,494
General Synod of the Evangelical Lutheran Church in the United States of America	270,221
United Synod of the Evangelical Lutheran Church in the South	47,747
General Council of the Evangelical Lutheran Church in North America	462,177
Evangelical Lutheran Synodical Conference of America	648,529
United Norwegian Lutheran Church in America	185,027
Evangelical Lutheran Joint Synod of Ohio and Other States	123,408
Hauge's Norwegian Lutheran Synod	33,268
Evangelical Lutheran Synod of Iowa and Other States	110,254
Synod for the Norwegian Evangelical Lutheran Church in America	107,712
Norwegian Lutheran Free Church	26,928
Other Lutherans (14 bodies)	97,223
MENNONITE BODIES	54,798
METHODIST BODIES	5,749,838

Denomination	Number of Members
Methodist Episcopal Church	2,986,154
Methodist Protestant Church	178,544
Methodist Episcopal Church, South	1,638,480
Free Methodist Church of North America	32,838
African Methodists	869,710
African Methodist Episcopal Church	494,777
African Methodist Episcopal Zion Church	184,542
Coloured Methodist Episcopal Church	172,996
Other African Methodists (4 bodies)	17,395
Other Methodists (4 bodies)	44,112
PRESBYTERIAN BODIES	1,830,555
Presbyterian Church in the United States of America	1,179,566
Cumberland Presbyterian Church	195,770
United Presbyterian Church of North America	130,342
Presbyterian Church in the United States	266,345
Other Presbyterians (8 bodies)	58,532
PROTESTANT EPISCOPAL CHURCH	886,942
REFORMED BODIES	449,514
Reformed Church in America	124,938
Reformed Church in the United States	292,654
Christian Reformed Church	26,669
Hungarian Reformed Church in America	5,253
SWEDISH EVANGELICAL BODIES	27,712
UNITARIANS	70,542
UNITED BRETHREN BODIES	296,050
Church of the United Brethren in Christ	274,649
Church of the United Brethren in Christ (Old Constitution)	21,401
UNIVERSALISTS	64,158
OTHER PROTESTANT BODIES	164,287
ROMAN CATHOLIC CHURCH	12,079,142
JEWISH CONGREGATIONS	101,457
LATTER-DAY SAINTS	256,647
Church of Jesus Christ of Latter-day Saints	215,796
Reorganized Church of Jesus Christ of Latter-day Saints	40,851
EASTERN ORTHODOX CHURCHES	129,606
Greek Orthodox Church	90,751
Other Eastern Orthodox Churches (3 bodies)	38,855
SPIRITUALISTS	35,056
ALL OTHER BODIES	46,655

V

THE MAKING OF THE SECTS

THE exuberance of sect-life in the United States is exactly what any sociologist would expect. With such ideal conditions it would be contrary to the trends of history if only one great church spread over the states. Nowhere, in all history, have social conditions favoured the growth of sects as they do now and here; and, though the conditions themselves are not the direct cause of the sects, any more than the absence of the gardener is the cause of the spread of undergrowth in the garden, still such conditions as are found here are the most conducive to sect formation.

Of course the most direct producer of variety in church organization is immigration. From all parts of the civilized world lines of pilgrims stream to this country, bringing with them their own faith, which has taken on the fashion of their particular social life and racial nature. Here they may retain, throughout all time, the characteristics which belonged to their former home. No official pressure is brought to bear upon them to direct them into an established church. So the "Religious Liberty," of which everyone who has caught the spirit of the New World is champion, may justly be considered the guardian of the sects. For not only does it welcome all comers from abroad, but it is equally hospitable to all additions to denominational families here. Such additions are to be expected. One of the first lessons of sociology shows that new ideas, philosophies, schools, social movements, grow up where the population is not homogeneous, but where people of various cultures mingle. So the great water courses in ancient times were the seats of civilization. For along the Tigris, the Euphrates, the Nile, among the islands of the Ægean Sea, the ships and people of many places would meet and exchange ideas and customs as well as merchandise. This ancient principle is at work to-day. No other nation shows such versatility, such prodigality of invention, such a profusion of social movements. This restless, progressive spirit, however, does not affect Christianity as much as might be expected. It does encourage numerous leaders to start innovations occasionally, and such leaders are allowed all the latitude they demand. It does keep the mind alert and incites the vigorous to protest against "wrongs," real or fancied. It does make for a toleration of opposing beliefs, which cannot be found in an old country where the population has remained homogeneous and the conventions of centuries rest upon the people. It is the spirit of a new country, where there is room for all comers and all opinions. Not an unmixed blessing are the sects incubated in so genial an atmosphere.

As has been said, such a spirit and such incentives will not explain the actual origin of the 186 sects. As a historical fact, the several nations which sent explorers to America in the sixteenth century are the forbears of the sects. Spain led the vanguard. She sent missionaries with her explorers. They established church centres everywhere they went. This was to be a Roman

THE MAKING OF THE SECTS

Catholic country. When a little band of Scotch-Irish Presbyterians ventured to settle in a Spanish domain, it was speedily obliterated with the sword. Had this sort of intolerance continued, and had the Spaniards spread their domain north as well as west, there could have been no sects. With the coming of the English, Dutch and Scotch-Irish, a number of the denominations which issued from the Reformation found footholds here in colonial times. Fortunately, the country was large enough for all. Had it been so small that Puritan, Baptist and Quaker were forced to be near neighbours, it is probable that only the strongest would have survived.

From colonial days to the present, the differences of nationality have been one of the most prolific causes of sectarianism. Differences of language, forms of worship, systems of doctrine, are almost invariably involved. Even where the church doctrine, practice and heritage are the same, as in the Roman Catholic Church, differences of language will call for different services; and in many Catholic communities, where the languages are not a source of separation, a natural attraction for like to like, a "consciousness of kind" often separates one people from another. The French wish a Church of their own, and the Irish do not want the Italians. Out of the friction the Catholic Church loses many adherents, though her skill in managing the situation is born of long practice. After a generation has passed and the children of the foreigner have gone through the American schools, these national antipathies disappear. If the jealousies and animosities, which so easily grow up between different people of different languages and traditions, could be wisely handled through one generation, the great cause of disruption would vanish. For the intermarrying and the levelling down of social intercourse reduce the artificial differences of nationality to something like a uniformity. Those genuine racial traits which remain, however, will not disappear, except after several generations of intermarrying. On the other hand, when factions grow up before the Americanizing influences get in their good work, the organizations started tend to perpetuate themselves, passing down to successive generations sects which originated from a situation that no longer exists. Thus are the sects of the fathers visited upon the children long after the third and fourth generations.

Nothing was more natural than the drifting apart of different national stocks in the growth of the great Lutheran Church, though the splendid work of Muhlenberg shows the possibilities of resisting such a natural drift. In the beginning of the eighteenth century there were a number of congregations of Dutch, Swedish and German Lutherans scattered through New York, New Jersey, Pennsylvania and Maryland. Each was jealous of its rights and privileges and tenacious of its independence. Muhlenberg succeeded in working these various, dissimilar churches into one great organization, despite the great obstacles of language, separate interests, race prejudices and separation by great distances. As years went on, the various churches used English more and more, their interests became identified, the older forms of thought and custom which were identified with their foreign homes became more uniform and took the character of their new environment. A great American church was the outcome. Unfortunately, issues arose which later resulted in secessions. Nevertheless, the heroic work of the men who brought the straggling, colonial churches into one great brotherhood stands as a precedent and an inspiration, and presents the great issue of church unity squarely before the twenty-four bodies of the Lutheran Church of to-day. What was done nearly two centuries ago under the most adverse circumstances, could surely be accomplished on a far grander scale to-day. The Lutheran churches have much in common. They have very much the same creeds, doctrines and traditions. They have the high honour of carrying the name of the founder of Protestantism. It is a stain upon their page in Christian history that they cannot bring their Norwegian, Danish, Swedish, German and Finnish brethren into one church, as they become citizens of one and the same nation.

The Reform churches, like the Lutheran, owe their diversity mainly to national differences, and, like the Lutheran, they should be able to organize much more closely than they do at present. One of the reasons for maintaining the characteristics of a sect which had its origin in national differences, is isolation. Thus the Dunkers were very largely farmers in colonial times, and their faith spread in rural districts, with the result that they have changed very little up to the present time, and wish to change still less.

To-day the immigration from countries where the Eastern Orthodox Church, i.e., the Greek Church, is dominant, is producing Russian, Servian, Syrian and Greek Orthodox churches. Closely allied to the schisms which grow out of national differences, are those divisions in the Christian church which grow out of racial differences. Many writers do not draw a sharp line between racial and national distinctions; they frequently use the words interchangeably. In the present instance, we shall mean by racial merely the Indian and African as contrasted with the white races. Among the Indians, the spread of Christianity presents a very interesting psychological study. The way in which the Catholic Church converted the Indian, and the resultant Indian Catholicism, is an interesting example of the possibilities, or perhaps we should say the impossibilities, of imposing one type of Christianity upon an uncivilized people. Of course, a similar situation appears where Protestantism has spread among the Indians. It would seem that different tribes, with different possibilities of civilization, are appealed to differently by the different sects.

Before the war the negroes worshipped in the churches of the whites; they frequently occupied seats in the galleries of the churches where their masters worshipped. After the war, when the relations between the whites and the blacks were seriously changed, the negro began to establish churches of his own. These churches have grown splendidly. It is a pity that they did not grow into one organization. The Methodists have five divisions running through their coloured churches. The next largest body of coloured worshippers is the Baptists. Between the Baptists and the Methodists there are a number of differences such as church government, ritual and minor points in doctrine; but these hardly outweigh what they have in common, especially among the negro churches. For the negro type of religious life is so thoroughly characteristic of his race, and differs so little among his kind, that the differences which grew up in the sects of the white man have little significance for him. Surely, if there is a people to whom one general

THE MAKING OF THE SECTS

type of church worship is congenial, these Afro-Americans are that people.

If the two former causes of disunion, nation and race, are due to an act of God, then truly the cause we are about to study is due to an act of Satan. Fifty years ago the nation fought out the question of disunion. Long before the first gun was fired, the issue had arisen in the churches. There the nation had a right to witness the great questions discussed in a Christian spirit. The bitterness which ran through the country should have stopped at the doors of the Church. It did not. Christianity as represented by the sects of that day proved pitifully incapable of coping with the problems of the nation. The Church failed to lead the nation in paths of peace. Surely that was a bad enough failure, but to be leaders in disunion and antagonism was immeasurably worse. That was a discreditable chapter in church history. It is not so ugly as the chapters written and being written since. Long ago the country was reunited, but the churches are still divided, presenting the spectacle of the perpetuation through generations of an animosity which the world has forgotten, but which still rankles in the Church. Men who fought against each other in the Civil War fought together against a common enemy thirty years later, but the churches of Christ which opposed each other in the sixties, continued to send out missionaries to compete with each other forty years after Lee surrendered. We saw in the last chapter how the Northern and Southern branches of one church were fighting each other, rather than a common enemy, in our own Northwest. Is it any wonder that leadership has passed out of the hands of the Church?

Into what sort of a calamity would a nation fall led by a church actuated with such a spirit?

The obstacles which tend to prevent the reunion of over two million Methodists in the North with nearly a million and a half in the South, are difficulties which these great bodies could surely overcome, if they were animated by as moving a spirit for Christian union as they were by the war spirit of a generation ago. The same may be said of the Baptist Church, with nearly two millions of worshippers in the South and nearly a million in the North. What a magnificent army these churches would present if they marched together! If they took the initiative, it is probable that many of the other divisions occasioned by the Civil War would be healed. The " Presbyterian Church in the United States," which sought to be the Presbyterian Church in the Confederated States, would probably be truer to its name if the spirit of union and self-denial for the great cause of Christ became widespread throughout its churches in the country. Indeed, the first step toward strengthening the Church, that it may regain its place among the great forces that direct the nation, would seem to be in a reunion of these long-severed family ties.

Another cause of disruption is in the Church itself; it grows out of differences in methods of administration. Church government or polity has occasioned a number of different forms of church organization. This particular type of disruption has not played a very prominent part in the making of the sects in America; though it has been very influential in the history of the Church elsewhere. Time was when the question, whether a pope, a bishop or a presbyter should administer the affairs of the Church, presented an issue of the very greatest importance. The great forms of church government were fairly well established before Christianity spread to America. Perhaps America's greatest contribution is one which grows out of the spirit of the country, and gives to each individual church an independence which is impossible in those polities which grew up in monarchical countries.

Occasionally in the history of the American Church, a rebellion has occurred against a too-rigid church government. The Methodist Protestant Church took issue with its parent body upon the question of representation in the conference by lay members, with the result that this difficulty of our great-grandsires presents us with a sect of nearly two hundred thousand members to-day. Sometimes the grievances of a minority are real, sometimes they are fancied. Now and then a union of churches occurs when churches of similar polity agree; as in the case of the Associate Synod and the Associate Reform Synod, which constitute the United Presbyterian Church of North America.

Although church polity is not an important cause of rupture in the United States, it is a very important factor in preventing the union of the churches. It is very difficult in many cases to alter the administration of the Church; offices must be abolished, church societies must be changed and a general rearrangement of the organization must be made. Perhaps it would not be fair to say that much of the resistance comes from those holding offices, from secretaries of societies, and men employed in educational, publication or other activities of the Church. But it is certainly true that the great movement for church coöperation must come from the intelligent and determined laymen. When the thirty million people who worship in the numerous sects of this country determine that matters of church government shall not separate them, it will not be long before polity will disappear as an argument against unity.

Though America may not present many varieties of church polity as sources of sectarianism, it can boast a number of remarkable leaders in the church history of the last century, whose efforts have built up sects containing hundreds of thousands of worshippers. In the first half of the nineteenth century, William Miller persuaded a number of his impressionable countrymen that the day of judgment was at hand and the numerous Adventist sects were the result. Joseph Smith, a native of Vermont, began to have visions concerning the second coming of Christ when he was fifteen years of age; other visions followed which were recorded in the Book of Mormon. These formed a basis for a new sect. In more recent times, Mrs. Eddy and John Alexander Dowie succeeded in inducing many people to accept their convictions. Mrs. Eddy has over eighty-five thousand followers. These last two sects had little to say about the second coming of Christ. They based their claims upon practical achievements. It would be impossible to start a great denomination among the churches to-day upon any doctrine concerning the second coming of Christ. Doctrinal interests are not in the spirit of the times. To-day the stress of life, especially in our large cities, is so severe that many people break down and suffer ill health primarily from nervous disorders. Any means of strengthening their hold upon life is eagerly sought. Such a means the followers of Mrs. Eddy and Mr. Dowie profess to possess. This is one of the reasons why the Christian Science Church has a larger proportion of members in the *cities* than any other sect.

By far the most important cause of the divisions in the sects among the Protestant churches is the spirit of protest. This gave birth to Protestantism; indeed, it gave birth to Christianity. Protestantism, whether in the time of Christ, or in the time of Luther, or in the time of the Puritans, is always actuated by the same spirit. It seeks to supplant the barrenness and the inefficiency of the religion of its time with something better. This spirit of protest may express itself in several ways; very frequently it seeks to find the better life by recurring to the past. It is a characteristic of human nature to hark back to the Golden Age of long ago. This is a trait of the individual memory, which always recalls the years of early life as the most beautiful of all the years; and it is a trait of humanity, which loves to point back to the achievements of past history. So the Church often looks back upon the achievements of the Apostolic Age, or the Reformation.

In the growth of the American sects there are many innovations made in this way. Thus the Primitive Baptists could not endure the worldly spirit which incited man to establish missions, benevolent societies and Sunday-schools! They sought the simple ways of the earlier Church. To-day their action does not seem reasonable. However, such an action is sometimes taken after mature deliberation, after a sober protest against the encroachments of worldly interests in the Church; and may, occasionally, be justified; though it would appear to be the part of wisdom and Christianity to reform the Church from within, rather than to add another sect to the already too-long list.

One of the largest sects in the country, the General Council of the Evangelical Lutheran Church of North America, arose some years ago, when a number of the members of the Lutheran Church felt that they were drifting from the historical moorings of their church. They started a movement to conserve the spirit of the earlier Church. They felt that the spirit of the earlier Lutherans had been changed in the mutations of modern life, and to bring back the vigour and vitality of the earlier Church they sought to return to its doctrines and customs.

It does not seem to matter in what period of church history a protest occurs. It always can find a more remote period as an ideal. Menno Simon sought to lead his fellows to the simpler Christianity of the early Church. That was back in the seventeenth century. From this came the Mennonite Church. After some years, one Ammon sought to bring the Mennonite Church back to the simplicity of Simon's teachings. From this came the Amish Mennonite Church. Again, in the seventeenth century, the Pietists sought to bring the vigour of primitive Christianity into a rather barren Protestant Church. From this movement came the "Dunkers" or the "German Baptist Brethren." They sought to resist modern influences, and to return to the spirit of the past, and gave rise to the Old Order of German Baptist Brethren. Much the same history explains the appearance of the "Friends" and the "Primitive Friends." The one division from the Disciples of Christ, the Churches of Christ, was inspired by this same desire to return to a simpler religious life. So, too, the United Evangelical Church, in the latter part of the nineteenth century, sought to go back to the doctrine, spirit and purpose of the earlier life of its parent church. The Free Methodist Church of North America arose from an agitation against the "worldly" Church of the early part of the nineteenth century. A number of smaller bodies, the Plymouth Brethren and the River Brethren, not to mention many others, have repeated these performances on a smaller scale.

Akin to this spirit, which seeks the betterment of the Church by a return to past principles and practices, is a spirit which also seeks the betterment of the Church, but does so regardless of the past. It is a more virile spirit. It usually grows out of the enthusiasm from a great revival; it is almost inevitably the product of some stirling spiritual movement.

As there is a trait in human nature which constantly looks to the past and extols those halcyon days, so there is a trait, in a great number of men, which looks to the future for the Best. This is not characteristic of religious people alone, but it is that characteristic of all men of all times which has divided them into conservatives and radicals. Every government of every country shows these two forces. History is one long succession of the results of their conflicts. In the Church the radical nature, when stirred with the enthusiasm of the religious spirit, is not long in seeking "*novas res.*"

In the eighteenth century, the revival started by Whitefield put new life into the churches. In some cases, an entire sect was stimulated. In some cases, a minority of the churches of a sect responded to the revival influences. In the latter "Old and New Light" would shine with varying degrees of lightness or dimness, or, a portion of the sect, unable to live comfortably with its fellows, would break off and form a new sect. In such a way the Free Baptists came into being. The Great Revival, in the early part of the nineteenth century, after the depression following the Revolutionary War, occasioned many changes in the churches. The Cumberland Presbyterian Church could not endure the dearth of spirituality of the Presbyterian Church, and sought freedom and a new life in a separate denomination. This same general movement affected a number of devout and capable men and occasioned the up-springing of a number of churches which have since become great and strong. The Disciples of Christ, the Primitive Methodists, the Christian Connection, the Evangelical Association, are among the churches that took their origin directly or indirectly from this great movement a century ago.

In the last decade of the nineteenth century a rather sporadic movement has appeared. It, too, takes the form of a revival of religious spirit. It is rather radical and eccentric, and gives rise to " various orders of Holiness Movements." It is a protest against the worldliness of the Church to-day, and an emphasis upon unique religious experiences.

Another source of eruption in the Church is differences in doctrine. These differences are not developed in the United States as much as is often imagined. Of course the distinctly American contributions are those from Miller, Smith, Eddy, Channing, Ballou, Dowie and a few others, which have already been noted. The great doctrinal forces, which grew up after the Reformation, have come over to America, and are reflected in the creeds of many of the churches. No great American thinker and leader has formulated a body of distinctive doctrines, which have given rise to any great family of denominations. In America, the sects seem rather to take their origin in differences of religious experience than in differences of thought. The Universalist and the Unitarian churches are products of theoretical movements. They have been very influential, but they have not spread extensively.

Theology does not appear to be a very important cause of sect origin; it is, nevertheless, a very great deterrent of church union. With the spread of education, many of the differences in doctrine are being levelled down, and it is not unreasonable to hope that in time devout and intelligent men may be able to agree upon the great fundamentals of Christianity.

Beneath many of these causes of separation lies a deeper cause. It is the natural difference between man and man in the thoughts and feelings which go into the shaping of the religious life itself. Such differences are inherent in human nature. It is impossible to ignore them. As each individual works out his own intellectual life, influenced by others, so, too, does he build up his religious conceptions and seek his religious development under the influence of others. His native promptings, plus these influences, give the direction of his religious life. No two human beings would be at all alike in their religion, were it not for the mutual influence upon each other's thoughts and feelings. So, different types of religious nature are drawn together by the assistance rendered each other in developing the spiritual life. These natural types are the bases of several great sect-types, as we shall see later.

VI

CLASSES OF SECTS

FROM the groups of causes which have operated to produce the sects, it may be argued that the sects themselves can be grouped according to their various characteristics. For the influences which give rise to new sects do not cease their activity with the birth of a sect, but continue to give direction to the new organization for generations. Thus a religious body which originated in a widespread revival, continues its course with much of the warmth of spirit and fervour of expression that gave it birth; another denomination, whose beginning is traced to a doctrinal distinction and to a stand upon positive convictions in theoretical matters, often continues in the doctrinal way; while a third sect rises from the peculiar views of some one man who stamps his personality and his principles upon his followers, and these run through the life of his organization; still another sect will arise out of an issue connected with some feature of church worship, and the life of the sect becomes unique in some ritual. So, the origin of a sect is a very good index of its general character, and we may well attempt a classification of the sects, based primarily upon this study of their origins.

Of course a large number of sects have their inception in matters wholly external to their religious life; of such are the sects formed by the issues of the Civil War, the divisions due to controversies over church government, or over the administration of educational institutions, etc. Only when the issue turns upon matters directly connected with the religious life of the members, can the origin tell anything of the nature of a sect. Those sects, considered in the last chapter, which sprang from distinctly religious needs, may be grouped according to the traits they have in common. In such a grouping it is impossible to draw broad and clear lines between the bodies classified, for one church may resemble another in many particulars, but, also, resemble a third in a few other features. For this reason, we shall use the origins of the sects only as a general index of their characters, and we shall consider their careers, their inner lives, also, in making an estimate of their positions in the classification.

One of the first things which attract the attention of the sociologist in a study of the people of America, is the distinctive trait which each nationality contributes to the complexion of the nation. Such traits arise in many ways; they may be due to genuine differences in the national stocks, or they may be due to peculiarities incident to social or natural environments. If they are due to environments which have operated upon the people for only a few generations, they will probably disappear. If they go deeper and run back to fundamental characteristics, they last for a very long time. These differences show themselves in a number of ways—in the kind of work which these people undertake when they come to a new country, in their social customs and forms of amusement, their personal morals, and especially in their religion, which is one of the most conservative factors in life. The Reformation took hold upon the peoples of northern Europe; it was congenial to them. The soil of their nature yielded fruit a hundredfold; but in the south of Europe the Reformation could not gain headway, and the principles of Protestantism never took root. Some reasons for this we have seen in a former chapter; certain minor differences are very apparent to the psychologist in the art, the literature, the music and the habits of the people of northern and southern Europe. These fundamental differences do not appear so clearly as you pass from nation to nation, as they do when you pass from the brachycephalic heads of the south to the dolichocephalic heads of the north. That the shape of the head shapes the religion no one can believe, but that the shape of the head goes with a number of other traits, among them religious traits, may very well be possible. A genuine difference exists between the people in the north and the people in the south of Europe, and it appears in their religion. In America it is natural to expect a recurrence of this phenomenon, and we may well look for some characteristic which marks the sturdy stock which made the Reformation.

A number of denominations in this country trace their history back to the people immediately affected by Luther's influence. Their lineage is not only doctrinal but human. For the very people who responded to Luther were the ancestors of many who stoutly defend his name to-day. The Lutheran Church is the greatest Protestant church in the world. The Lutheran Church in America would be one of the largest, if it were not divided into twenty-four divisions. Nevertheless, through these divisions one may see certain characteristics in common. The first is that all of these separate bodies look back to the Augsburg Confession as the constitution of their faith. Some of them accept in addition Luther's catechism, or the Smalkald Articles; or perhaps also the Apostolic, the Nicene or the Athanasian creeds. Their central doctrine is salvation through faith in Christ, and their theology turns upon that. They are a people who retain the doctrinal tenets of the past, but have also a religious experience which runs parallel with their doctrines. They are neither as doctrinal as the Presbyterian, nor as insistent upon the spiritual experience as the Methodist; but doctrine and devotion of a characteristic kind run through them all, despite national differences (see page 195).

Nearly three hundred thousand members of the Reformed Church in the United States, formerly the German Reformed Church, also trace their religion back to the inspiration of the Reformation. Their constitution, if we may so call the doctrinal expression of the church, is in the Heidelberg catechism. This statement of faith, like many others of the period of its making, reflects the same general principles that are contained in the Augsburg Confession. The religious life of these followers of Luther is very much like that of the Lutherans. Indeed, with the religious life centring around the same ideas and taking its colour from the same racial temperament, it is hard to see why these two bodies should remain distinct.

The German Evangelical Synod, which also has nearly three hundred thousand members, retains the Augsburg Confession and the Heidelberg catechism, both as the religious expressions of its life. It would seem possible, then, that all these German descendants of the Great Reform could have the same doctrinal basis for their faith. The minor issues which a theologian might take exception to mean nothing to the average layman. The general tenets of a belief are all that influence the average worshipper. Here the general tenets are the same. Not only so, but the spiritual experience which runs along with these general convictions, takes much the same form in these people whose thought and ancestry run back to one origin.

Here, then, we have a group of sects which might well be called a type. Of course there are many exceptions to the average, and minor diversities certainly appear in the Danish, the Finnish, or the Norwegian branches. One sect reflects a principle we find in many places. Among the Norwegian Lutherans a sect, under Hauge, sprang up in protest against the barrenness of the spiritual life; it lays more emphasis upon spirituality, and none upon creed. With the rank and file of these millions of worshippers, the general traits of their stock, in temperament, in belief and in worship, remain the same.

Among other national strains in the great composition of the American people, preference for certain forms of the Christian religion may also be traced. The Scotch-Irish stock, with its stalwart qualities; the Irish, so different in temperament; the English and the Dutch; not to mention a number of others, have given their trend to the sect-making. Still, these people are not to be compared with the Teuton, in their influence upon the church history of America. For they have been more susceptible to the influences which drew them into sects not bound by characteristics of nationalities.

A very distinct group of race-sects is that comprised of negroes. Here there are very marked race characteristics, for the African race is well removed. Its temperament, its intellectual life, its emotional nature, its many primitive traits, all mark it off from the Caucasian. Matters of doctrine play very little part in the religion of the negro, except as they stir his imagination. The emotional nature is the actuating factor of his religion. Negro Unitarians are almost impossible. Indeed, all of those sects that have laid great emphasis upon the intellectual factors in religion, have made little appeal to the negro. The Presbyterian Church was not so much weaker than the Methodist and the Baptist before the war, but the Presbyterian Church, with its love of doctrine, has succeeded in sending comparatively few of the negroes to its altars, while the Baptists, with their insistence upon a regenerated heart rather than a regenerated mind, have won many of the negroes. Indeed, 61 per cent. of membership of all the coloured organizations is in the Baptist Church, 13 per cent. in the Methodist, and one-eighth of 1 per cent. in the Presbyterian. Whatever may be said of difference in efforts on the part of these churches to reach the negro, whatever discount may be made for their differences in size, it still remains to be explained why so few coloured people are in the Presbyterian Church, and so many in the Baptist and the Methodist. Surely, part of the explanation is in the fact that these two churches more nearly satisfy the negro's religious needs. There are greater differences between the negro churches and the white churches than there are between the different sects in the negro church. With the education and cultivation of the negro, the excesses which used to characterize his worship will disappear; but his real religious needs will remain the same, in great measure. He should not be forced to fashion his church life after that of the white man, but should be encouraged to establish one great church having sufficient variety of forms of worship to satisfy him, and to develop along lines most congenial to his nature.

In the study of the origins of the sects, we saw that the great religious revival which swept over the country, gave rise to divisions in the old churches and to the birth of new churches. Here, then, we have an appeal to the spiritual nature as the supreme incentive for forming a church. The response to this appeal came from those people who found the experience of religion a supreme factor in their lives. Theology had little to do with it. Doctrine was ignored; only the great central principles of Christianity were considered. In the religious awakening in the early part of the nineteenth century, the people who responded gave little thought to the theoretical differences of the different churches; they were absorbed in the great ethical and spiritual issues of the moment. We saw that the Disciples of Christ, the Evangelical Association, the "Christians," and the Cumberland Presbyterian Church, and we might add the "Winebrennerian," originated in this movement. Now, if we study the after-careers of these churches, we shall find that they have very much in common. The Disciples take this position: "While agreeing with all the Evangelical churches in the necessity of faith and repentance, we differ in this: we submit no other tests but faith and repentance in admitting persons to baptism and church membership. We present to them no articles of faith other than the one article concerning the divinity and Christhood of Jesus. . . . They are wedded to Christ and not to a set of doctrines

CLASSES OF SECTS 83

or to a party." * This church insists only upon a religious experience which makes for Christian living; it holds forth no creeds; it seeks the unity of all churches. The Evangelical Association has a like spirit: " There is nothing radical in our creed, we hold a common faith of Orthodox Christians." † In addition to the Articles of Faith of the Methodist Church, which constitute in general the belief of the Church, the Evangelical Association holds to an adoption of Christian perfection. " Christian perfection is defined as a state of grace, in which we are so firmly rooted in God that we have instant victory over every temptation the moment it presents itself, without yielding in any degree; in which our rest, peace and joy in God are not interrupted by the vicissitudes of life. . . . Yet no perfection of experience is attainable that does not admit of higher and deeper and fuller participation in the infinite fulness of divine peace, life and power, but a constant expansion of spiritual capacity and enlargement of faith." The " Christians," or Christian Connection, also hold the Bible is the only source of their belief, and they have no need for a creed. Christian character is the only test of church fellowship. They, too, welcome church unity and the fellowship of all who share the Christian religion. The Cumberland Presbyterian Church, coming from a theological stock, carried as much of the Westminster faith with them as they could; some of it they could not carry. Their hearts had been stirred by a great experience, and the old doctrines of Calvinistic predestination did not fit their experience. So we

* B. B. Tyler: " A History of the Disciples of Christ," p. 122.
† S. O. Sprang: " A History of the Evangelical Association," p. 420, Vol. XII in the American Church History Series.

find this branch of the Presbyterian Church tending to hold to the Arminian doctrine of free will. However, this product of the great awakening in the religion of the nineteenth century also lays very little emphasis upon doctrine. It does not require subscription to the confession of faith by those who wish to join the church. These traits, which grew up as a result of the revival, became more common in the parent Presbyterian body as time went on, so that a reunion between the two was not impossible. The last church which we shall consider that grew out of this movement, is the Winebrennerian. Here, too, no written creed is required. The doctrine, so far as there is any doctrine, is Arminian rather than Calvinistic. The great emphasis is upon regeneration of heart and genuine practical piety.

In this group of churches we have a set of common characteristics. They grew out of a movement which demanded a religious experience rather than a doctrinal belief or a subscription to one form of worship and ritual. They have continued to hold to these principles. They constitute a very large portion of the Christian churches in the United States. They have so much in common, and are so willing to fraternize with all who have a similar " witness of the Spirit," that it seems improbable that they should long remain separated by the less important traits of church polity.

Another group of sects might also be called experiential. In these churches the emphasis is upon the spiritual life. If we were to draw a sharp distinction, we should say that it is a feeling element in religion, rather than an intellectual element, which is the more emphasized among these sects. That feeling element is very different in the Quaker and the Methodist. One is at one end of the keyboard and the other at the opposite extreme. To pass from the quiet, subtle promptings of the Spirit in the demure Quaker to the racking, explosive demonstrations of the camp meeting, is to pass down the gamut of religious feeling. It is what one feels within that stirs him to express himself; his expression is directed by that stirring. Somewhere on that gamut, we should have to find a place for the Baptist, who knows when he is regenerated; for the member of the Salvation Army, who knows when he is converted; for the "Holiness" Christian, who knows when he has been sanctified, or perfected, and for many others. Now, surely, the historical differences in the origins of these sects give some indication of the traits which have always characterized them; but we should be led astray if we looked only to the origins.

Another great group with a very distinctive characteristic we might entitle the "*Doctrinal Group.*" In these churches doctrines have played a preëminent part. Among them the Presbyterian holds high rank. Originating as it did in the genius of Calvin, it has strongly adhered to that genius. It is the genius of logic. Calvin's "Institutions" were all written before he reached the age when Jesus began His public ministry. They were not based upon a life of religious experience; they were based upon close-knit logical reasoning. Calvin was a man with very little feeling. He preached a rigid doctrine and taught a rigid ethical system. The fervour of the Methodists had no part in his system. Taking an impression from the strong logical intellect of John Calvin, it always has put theoretical doctrine into its foreground. It has laid a stress upon doctrinal soundness as an element of wholesome church life, which defends it from both Lutheran and Anglican Protestantism. Its weaker side, in this respect, has been an overconfidence in the adequacy of human logic, to bring the truth of the Scriptures into a systematic form, and to present a doctrinal scheme which the Bible does not furnish. Closely akin to the spirit of the Presbyterian Church was the spirit of the Congregational churches for many generations. This was preëminently the church of New England, where there arose a number of great thinkers, who have given us a New England theology. In these later years the Congregational churches have worked away from their doctrinal bias, but are still among the leaders in the religious thought of to-day. So similar were the Congregational and Presbyterian churches in their intellectual life a century ago, that their ministers passed from the pulpits of one sect to the other freely. It was felt that these two denominations were very close together. From the Congregational the Unitarians separated upon a theoretical question, whose roots run back many years in colonial history. The bitterness engendered by this has made the Congregational and the Unitarian churches appear to be very different in character. As time went on, the body which separated did the natural thing, insisted upon a certain form of intellectual statement of faith, which gave the sect an ultra-intellectualistic cast. The Universalist Church, another New England product, also had its inception in a revolt against Congregational theology. It, too, has claimed a disdain for the intricacies and deceptions of theology, but has, nevertheless, laid such emphasis upon its tenets that it has also taken much the same cast as the Unitarian.

Such churches laying the primary emphasis upon the

forms of thought, whether in creed or not, that express the religious life, and seeking to emphasize with this their ethical standards, constitute a distinctive type of sects.

Still another type of denominations appears in those churches which turn to the church service, to the ritual as the dominant factor in their Christianity. The Catholic Church emphasized the importance of the eucharist to such an extent that the mass became the most important thing in the church life. By means of the body and blood of the Saviour, mystically imparted to the believer, salvation was attained. Should it be impossible to administer the Sacraments of the Church, it would be impossible to maintain Christianity. These sacraments are the cornerstone of the Church. Under such a dispensation, one must attend the church service and receive from its ritual the means of maintaining his religious life. The Church, too, must hear his confessions, and through the Church must he receive his forgiveness. The Catholic Church is not a *help* to the religious life. It is an *indispensable means* to its followers. A very different class of men are attracted by its service from those who feel within themselves the ability to find their God, to know Him, to receive the assurance of His presence and His existence, independent of any institutes, and who use the Church as an auxiliary, not as an indispensable means to the religious life.

That group of sects, founded by different persons in America, such as Miller, Smith, Dowie, Eddy or Crowdy, might well constitute another type of sects. They all take their origin from some interpretation of the Scriptures. They over-emphasize some feature of Christianity; or they graft on some misinterpretation of the Scriptures and develop it according to their humour. Though these sects originated under the inspiration of some dominating personality, the things for which they stand are so dissimilar that it is necessary in drawing the line around them to draw it very loosely. They may be classed from the point of view of psychology in rather a different way from that in which their historical origin would class them.

These types of sects do not include all of the individual churches in the United States. There may be a church here and there which cannot find a place in one of these types. By far the great majority of them, however, may easily be placed in some one of the above classes. Such a sect as the Swedenborgian, for example, does not originate in America, and could not be grouped as an American sect arising from the inspiration of an American leader; but it is in many particulars similar to those sects which have so arisen, and have taken their stand upon the professed revelations of their leaders.

VII

THE NATURAL SECTS

TWO sets of influences give rise to the sects; external or circumstantial, and internal or natural. The latter alone is important, as the adventitious influences of the social order do not produce lasting effects, and sects formed by them may readily re-form into bodies which directly influence their religious preferences. The native disposition to worship, believe and act in certain ways is fundamental. To find what these fundamental traits are, in the religious nature, is one of the tasks the psychologist has undertaken. It is a large and difficult problem, one which invites pitfalls. At present only large trends may be pointed out. However, these trends are of great significance, and assist materially in acquiring a true understanding of the nature of the divisions which run through the American Church.

Dr. Jean du Buy has made a very interesting comparative study in the psychology of four different types of Protestants.* In it he shows some of the typical traits of the Presbyterian, the Baptist, the Methodist and the Unitarian. This he does by pointing out the characteristics of the founders of these sects, showing how these characteristics continue in the life of the organizations.

Dr. du Buy finds that the spirit of Calvin has been

* *Amer. Jour. of Relig., Psychol. and Educ.*, 3, pp. 165-209.

perpetuated in the Calvinistic churches. By the typical Calvinist he does not mean the average member of a present-day Presbyterian Church, but he means rather the characteristics of the laymen who were attracted to the movement when it was young. These main characteristics have been repeated in every genuine follower ever since. " The typical Calvinist is intellectual. Calvin himself was distinguished by an uncommonly clear and powerful intellect. The typical Calvinist dwelt on the intellectual side of religion. Calvinistic preaching was didactic, and was an appeal to the intellect rather than to feeling. The typical Calvinist is logical. Calvin's own mind was exceedingly clear and logical. He early formed a habit of arranging his thoughts logically, and of thus reducing them to order. The typical Calvinist is distinguished by his logical precision, as well as his keen analysis and sharp argumentation. The typical Calvinist is a systematizer of thought. Calvin himself had a genius for organizing thought. The typical Calvinist endeavours to erect a theological system by means of logical inference. His creed surpasses those of all other Protestants in systematical elaborateness. He is characterized by an over-confidence in the adequacy of logic to bring theological thought into a system. The typical Calvinist is an organizer by nature. Calvin himself had a genius for organizing. The typical Calvinist is a theologian. Calvin's main interest was in theology and in doctrinal soundness. The typical Calvinist puts theological doctrine into the foreground. He is distinguished by his fine-spun theological definitions. His interest in dogmatical theology is intense. He is more interested in doctrinal questions than all other Protestants. The typical Calvinist is dogmatic. Calvin himself was dogmatic. . . . The typical Calvinist is unemotional. Calvin himself was greatly lacking in emotion. He became early distinguished by a certain strictness and severity of character. . . . Calvinism has set up a high standard of intelligence both for its ministers and its laity. It stands for an educated ministry."

His study of the " Typical Methodist " brings out some sharp contracts with the " Typical Calvinist." " The religion of the Methodist is a religion based upon personal experience, on the experience of the forgiveness of our sins, on a sense of pardon of all past sins. Inseparably connected with this sense of pardon, is the new trust in God on the part of the convert. The typical Methodist insists that conversion be always preceded by an overwhelming sense of personal guilt, by what is called conviction of sin, and that it be followed by a joyful assurance of reconciliation with God. . . . A typical Methodist preacher demanded of a man's conversion that it be a conscious experience, usually involving a conscious submission to God. . . . Methodist revival preachers were even loath to recognize anyone as truly converted who had not experienced a large measure of emotional excitement. . . . The typical Methodist is neither dogmatic nor controversial. There have never been any radical divergencies of doctrine among American Methodists. True Methodist preachers have not cared for theological controversies, because they were completely absorbed in the work of the conversion and saving of souls. The typical Methodist is distinguished by his zeal and activity, he is indefatigable. . . . The typical Methodist is distinguished by a certain directness and aggressiveness. The typical Methodist is emotional. Early Methodism was a great outburst of religious feeling. Typical Methodist preaching is highly emotional. Wesley's preaching frequently excited ungovernable emotion in the hearts of many of his hearers. . . . The typical Methodist is distinguished by his powerful fervency and religious enthusiasm. He is characterized by a fervour of address in preaching. . . . The genuine Methodist is decidedly a man of prayers. . . . He is an enthusiastic singer of hymns. . . . The early converts to Methodism were mainly members of the lower classes. They were chiefly poor, uneducated and even rude people. Indeed, Wesley himself intended his work mainly for the benefit of the lower classes in society. . . . The typical Methodist is emotional. Methodism naturally appeals to people of an emotional temperament. Thus an emotional woman will find in the fervency of Methodist preaching a response to the longings of her own nature. There surely is such a thing as a Methodist type of temperament. There is no mistaking a typical Methodist for a Calvinist or a Unitarian."

The analysis of the Baptist is equally interesting, though it does not bring out psychological differences so clearly. "The most fundamental principle of the Baptists is their demand for an exclusively regenerate church membership. The typical Baptist draws a sharp line of distinction between the consciously regenerate and those who make no claim to a regenerative change. He believes in the necessity of regeneration, and demands that regeneration should precede church membership. He insists that a church must be composed exclusively of regenerate persons, of individuals who are assured of their conversion. He rejects infant baptism largely because it is incompatible with a regenerate church membership. . . . The typical Baptist may be a Calvinist or an Arminian in his theology. The Regular Baptists of America are Calvinists, but the Freewill Baptists of America are Arminian. A number of speculative thinkers among the Baptists have been Socinians and Anti-Trinitarians. The Regular Baptists of America have no creed to-day to which all of them have to subscribe. Submission to a creed is not a condition of membership in Baptist churches. The Bible is preëminently their creed. Neither Calvinistic doctrine nor any other theological view is one of the essential characteristics of the Baptists. The typical Baptist is an advocate of absolute liberty of conscience. He believes that religion is a personal concern, a matter between the individual man and God. . . . The typical Baptist is distinguished by a peculiar literalness in his interpretation of the New Testament. Like the Calvinist, he maintains the doctrine of the supremacy and the sufficiency of the Bible as the only norm of faith and practice. . . . The Baptists practise what they call 'believers' baptism,' that is, the baptism of adult believers. Repentance, or change of heart, and faith are the conditions upon which alone they baptize people. Those who profess repentance and faith are the only proper subjects of baptism, according to them. . . . Infants are not the proper subjects of baptism because they cannot experience the 'new birth'; the spirit of regeneration belongs to adult people."

The Unitarian stands out in rather sharp relief against these other types. ("Described in one word, Unitarianism is an appeal to reason and conscience. The typical Unitarian asserts the claim of reason in religion. He appeals to reason in the interpretation of the Bible. He insists that no religious doctrine which is contrary to reason should be accepted. He contends for the freedom of private criticism and of private interpretation, and is distinguished by independence of thought and by a tendency toward rationalism. The typical Unitarian is a person who wants to be unpledged to any prescribed theological doctrine. He does not recognize any creed, not even the simplest one, as binding him. . . . Has a strong dislike of dogma as well as of controversy. . . . Does not recognize the authority of any church discipline over him. . . . The typical Unitarian is unemotional. Non-Unitarians have often made the charge of lack of emotion against him. They speak of his cold intellectualism. They are of the opinion that the religious life of the Unitarian is wholly intellectual, without any demonstration; almost entirely of the head, very little of the heart. They regard him as highly respectable, but frigid in his piety. . . . Seems to be lacking in the religious life. Unitarianism appeals most strongly to people of culture. It finds its adherents largely in the cultivated class. The typical Unitarian is an educated and cultivated man who has some wealth and having a good social position. . . . Unitarianism has never been a religion for the masses, the latter require a religion which is more emotional, and which emphasizes the inward moral struggle against temptation and sin."

The most interesting thing from the point of view of psychology, in this study, is the distinction which appears between the Presbyterian and Unitarian on the one hand, and the Baptist and the Methodist on the other. This would seem to be due to native traits. The former, though wide apart theologically, are near together psychologically. Both Presbyterian and Unitarian are of the intellectual type as distinguished from the Baptist and Methodist, who lay more emphasis upon the experiential factors in religion. With the former two sects, the interest revolves around what is thought; with the latter two, their interest centres upon what is felt, experienced.

Professor Giddings makes a more elaborate study of the sects, and endeavours to classify all of them under five heads. He has the four following mental types.*

"*Idio-Motor.*—This is the lowest type of the human mind. Its activities are for the most part instinctive. Sensations, simple ideas and motor reactions are in this type not merely the materials out of which mind and practice-activity are built, as in higher types, but they are a chief content of conscious life. Intellect does not develop much beyond perception and conjecture. Belief is determined mainly by incident, habit and auto-suggestion. The disposition is aggressive and the character forceful. Examples are afforded by the lowest savages, and in several populations by the physically active but ignorant.

"*Idio-Emotional.*—This is somewhat weakly but almost continuously emotional rather than physically active. Its intellect is imaginative. Its beliefs are largely determined by external suggestions, and it habitually reasons from superficial analogy. It is instigative in disposition and convivial in character. Examples are afforded by all the higher savages and barbarians, and especially by the negroes. In civil populations the type is found in two gradations: one, the emotional volatile minds, not densely ignorant but of comparatively little

* F. H. Giddings: "Inductive Sociology," pp. 84-89.

intellectual development, and two, the sensuous, imaginative, artistically creative minds, of higher intellectual development.

"*Dogmatic-Emotional.*—This type is marked by an extreme development of preferential attention. The mind is fixed upon some one dominant idea or group of ideas or beliefs. Such controlling ideas arouse great volumes of emotion, which, in turn, create a habit of intolerance. Belief, in this type, is suggestively determined by emotion, movement and temperament. Reasoning is habitually deductive, and, while much nice attention may be given to the logical process, premises are seldom subjected to a searching criticism, but are usually accepted on trust. Disposition is domineering and character austere. Persons of this type have often been useful to the community as reformers or even as martyrs, but they are seldom temperate or judicious in their methods. . . .

"*Critical-Intellectual.*—The highest type of mind is that in which the Idio-Motor, the Idio-Emotional and the Dogmatic-Emotional activities, never suppressed, much less destroyed, are habitually kept under the control of a critical and vigilant intellect. Clear perceptions, sound judgments, objectively determined by evidence and taking the form of common sense, careful reasoning, deductive or inductive, a habit of subjecting premises no less than logical processes to a searching examination—these intellectual activities constitute a major part of the mental life, and keep all of the lower processes in due subordination. Intellect in this type may be deductive and critical, or critical and inductive. Disposition is creative and character rationally conscientious."

THE NATURAL SECTS

Using these types of mind Professor Giddings finds that the denominations fall in the following lists.*

DISTRIBUTION BY SECTS

Type of Mind	MIE. Ideo-Motor.	IM to IE.	EIM. Ideo-Emotional.	IE to DE.	IEM. Dogmatic-Emotional.	DE to CI.	IME. Critical-Intellectual.
Adventists	...	...	...	½	½	...	...
Baptists, white	...	...	⅛	¾	⅛	...	...
Baptists, coloured	...	...	1	...	...	...	...
Catholics	...	¼	½	¼	...	...	...
Catholic Apostolic	...	...	...	...	1	...	...
Christians	...	...	...	...	...	1	...
Christian Scientists	...	...	...	½	½	...	...
Congregationalists	...	...	...	...	...	1	...
Disciples of Christ	...	...	...	½	½	...	...
Dunkards	...	...	...	1	...	...	...
Evangelical Association	...	...	...	½	½	...	...
Friends	...	...	...	1	...	...	...
German Evangelical Prot.	...	...	...	...	1	...	...
German Evangelical Synod	...	...	...	¼	¾	...	...
Jewish Congregations	...	...	...	...	1	...	...
Latter-Day Saints	...	...	...	½	½	...	...
Lutherans	...	...	...	...	1	...	...
Mennonites	...	...	...	1	...	...	...
Methodists, white	...	...	⅛	¾	⅛	...	...
Methodists, coloured	...	...	1	...	...	...	...
Moravians	...	...	...	1	...	...	...
Presbyterians	...	...	...	...	¾	¼	...
Protestant Episcopalians	...	...	...	¼	½	¼	...
Reformed	...	...	...	...	¾	¼	...
Salvation Army	...	⅛	¼	½	⅛	...	...
Society for Ethical Culture	...	...	...	...	...	1	...
Spiritualists	...	...	...	1	...	...	...
Theosophical Study	...	...	...	...	1	...	...
Unitarians	...	...	...	...	...	1	...
Universalists	...	...	...	...	...	1	...
All Others	...	...	...	1	...	...	...

In this table the Baptists and the Methodists are classed together. They tend toward the Idio-Emotional.

*Psychol. Rev., 8, p. 345.

Seventy-five per cent. of them are between the Idio-Emotional and the Dogmatic-Emotional. The Unitarians are all grouped between the Dogmatic-Emotional and the Critical-Intellectual. Twenty-five per cent. of the Presbyterians are in the same class and 75 per cent. are in the Dogmatic-Emotional class.

The value of the table is this: It shows from the sociologist's point of view the sects as they group themselves in a progressive arrangement, passing from traits which are instinctive, automatic, to traits which are emotional, affective, and then to intellectual, deliberative traits.

We have already seen that Professor Pratt found five types of religious belief in his *questionnaire*. These would correspond in many particulars with the types above presented. For example, his first class was made up of those who believed in God from argument or reasoning, the intellectual element being dominant. His fourth class were characterized by a *desire* to believe, a matter of volition; and his fifth class were those whose religious belief arose from profound experiences,—they "felt" God. We have also seen that Professor Leuba agrees with these general positions, in that he groups religious philosophers into the three classes influenced by the intellect, the emotional or the volitional factors respectively.

Each of these four independent studies made by men interested in different phases of the subject bring out the same general facts. It is evident that the two distinctive traits in human nature, the intellectual and the emotional, are two poles around which other traits gather. If we spread the characteristics of the sects before us, they will fall into a plan which shows one of these poles

THE NATURAL SECTS 99

upon one side, the other upon the opposite side, and gradations shading from the one to the other in between.

It is not easy to turn to the denominations themselves and to say, " Here is a distinctively intellectual or emotional people," because in the present day the churches have so much in common. Cities exercise a large influence. Men who are engaged in the same sort of occupation, living the same sort of lives, reading the same newspapers, enjoying the same amusements, are very apt to worship in the same way. They have their thoughts trained in the same schools, they have their feelings aroused by much the same literature. They are levelled down. The Church helps in this process. The greater number of members in the churches come from the Sunday-school. In the Sunday-school there may be many different types of mind, but social pressure, the influence of others, the imitation of the example of other youths, all tend to sweep different types from the Sunday-school into the same church. This evil is partially remedied by adults seeking the most congenial church in later life; especially when they move from one locality to another. It is also true, unfortunately, that social prestige frequently persuades them from their genuine religious preference. Some people attend, and even join, the Church which has the highest local social standing. Nevertheless, if these religious traits are genuine, we shall expect to find them giving evidence of their existence in the sects. That there are in every community of any size whatever different types of mind, no one can doubt. This appears in many ways. A certain class of people prefer a certain type of newspaper, a certain kind of magazine, a certain class of theatres, a certain class of books from the public library, certain kinds of amusement, and, of course, a certain kind of church. It would be an interesting study to show the correlation between newspapers, theatres, books, amusements and sects.

Let us take two very dissimilar sects, both of American origin, both among people of some culture—the Unitarian and the Christian Science. The Unitarian has been described by Dr. du Buy. He is classed by Professor Giddings as one of the most intellectual and one of the least emotional. The Christian Scientist reasons in a very different way from the Unitarian. Into the Scientists' reasoning the "affective processes" enter with great power. Close-knit reasoning has no place in the Christian Science régime. The book which takes its place alongside of the Bible appeals not to a logical mind, but to an impressionable mind. It urges its theories by constant reiteration and a remarkable obscuration of logic. No scientist, no philosopher, no historian, would be convinced of the truth claimed by Christian Science from the argument sent forth. Only those who read the book or listen to the followers of Christian Science with a desire to better their physical health or change their spiritual life find its reasoning at all cogent. The cogency is due not to intellect, but to sympathetic feeling. There is the desire, the will to believe. It acts as the affective nature always acts upon the intellect, it distorts, prejudices. We shall expect to find among the Christian Scientists more people of an emotional type than among the Unitarians. Is there any way of making an analysis which would show the character of the two sects? There is an indirect test. We shall see later on that the type of mind which makes Christian Science possible is distinctly more feminine than the type of mind which issues in Unitarianism. So, then, we should expect to find a larger proportion of women in the Christian Science churches than in the Unitarian churches. And this is exactly what appears in the Census for Religious Bodies in 1906. Here it is shown that women outnumber men in all churches; but that the Unitarian Church averages fewer women than most of the others. There are 60.8 per cent. of women in the membership of the Unitarian Church and 72.4 per cent. in the Christian Science Church. This great difference cannot be due to chance. It is undoubtedly due to actual differences of religious type.

The statistics which show the proportion of women to men are influenced by a number of things. The proportion is different in different sections of the country. Different local influences will affect it also. It varies in churches of the same denomination in the same city. So it is a proportion that cannot tell us a great deal; but where so wide a difference appears as that we have just noticed, it is evidence of a fundamental native difference.

Another way of testing the same matter is afforded by this same census report. Instead of looking for emotional factors as evidences of differences in sects, we may look for traits indicative of the intellectual factor. In the ordinary walks of life, the intelligence of a community is gauged by certain objective results. If a people is intelligent, it shows. In a rough way, the material positions are an index of ability. "The fool and his money are soon parted." The more intelligence a man has, the larger his income will probably be. Of course, there are so many glaring contradictions to this excellent rule that many doubt its worth. Nevertheless, a little reflection will show that the untrained labourer cannot earn as much as the one who has learned a trade, nor does he who has just enough ability to earn a living in a trade earn as much as the professional man or the business man. This hard matter-of-fact gauge of men's ability may be used in our present study. Surely, the material possessions of the members of the several sects are some index of their place in the social order and of the intelligence which won them that place. In spite of the many exceptions to the rule, we may say that the wealthier churches are undoubtedly the more intellectual churches. The next question is how to gauge the wealth of the churches. It does not appear in the value of the church property. For churches which are in the cities would have the more valuable property. Nor does it appear in their benevolences, for the poor religionist may well be the more generous. It does appear, however, in the salaries which the members of the churches pay their ministers. This is an excellent index of the wealth of a church. For the salary is the least erratic expenditure which the church makes, and tells better than anything else the status of the church. Making such a comparison we have the following table.

AVERAGE SALARY OF MINISTERS

	Cities of 300,000	100,000-300,000	50,000-100,000	25,000-50,000	Outside Principal Cities
Unitarian	$2940	$2472	$2048	$1876	$1221
Presbyterian	2169	1896	1711	1524	977
Congregational	1938	1701	1764	1512	880
Protestant Episcopal	1873	1533	1558	1517	994
Baptist	1580	1420	1381	1248	683
Methodist	1422	1275	1207	1187	741
Disciples	1326	1313	1283	1250	526
Evangelical Association	812	774	738	668	568

This shows for eight churches, selected because of their distinctively American history and character, that the Unitarian and Presbyterian are both better off in this world's goods than the Methodist and Baptist.

Another way of attacking the same question is to compare the denominations which appeal to people living in the cities and to people living in the country. Again it may be maintained, in a large way, that the average city member has had a better education and ranks higher intellectually than the member of a country church. The statistics for illiteracy show a very much higher rate for the country than for the city. In the cities the opportunities for exchanging ideas are greater than in the country. Whatever vigour and virtue may come from the country to the city, the city still enjoys a preëminence of education and intelligence. If we select the same eight sects and compare their proportion of members in the country and in the city, we find a correspondence.* In this comparison the Protestant Episcopal Church has more members in her city churches than in the country churches: more exactly in the cities of 25,000 and over it has over 50 per cent.; falling in order of city membership are the Unitarian, the Congregational, the Presbyterian, the Evangelical, the Methodist, the Baptist and the Disciples. So, the four churches which lead the list in wealth are the four churches which have spread in the cities rather than the country, and the four churches which give their ministers the smaller salaries are the churches which have spread in the country. It might be argued that such churches as the Baptist and Methodist, with their great missionary zeal, have built more

* See p. 83 of Census Report for Religious Bodies, 1906.

churches in the country and have striven harder to win converts; but when a comparison is made of the number of communicants per church in these several denominations for all places of less than 25,000 inhabitants, it appears that the Presbyterian and Baptist have the same number of churches per member; so, too, with the Episcopalian and the Methodist, the Congregational and the Disciples. It is hardly a matter of missionary zeal, it is rather a matter of temperament. The more emotional type of Christianity appeals more to the man who does not earn his bread by his brain alone.

Statistics are very uncertain props to arguments. Like the Scriptures in the hands of the backwoods preacher, almost anything may be proved from them. However, the trends just noted seem so obvious that they certainly may be taken as corroborations of the characterizations made above.

It remains, therefore, to study the traits of human nature which give expression of themselves in these different religious preferences and organizations.

VIII

TYPES OF HUMAN NATURE

IN the opening chapters a number of facts connected with individuality and typical characteristics of human nature were discussed. In a general way it was seen that every person has his own mental and moral make-up, but that in all this individuality there may, also, be found a number of traits in common among men; so that it was possible to speak of types of men. Nothing was said concerning exactly what types of human nature may be found. It was merely pointed out that the average man classed his fellows in obvious types which were based upon practical matters. Such a classification grows up naturally in the intercourse between men; it is one of the conveniences of common sense. We have also seen that the *religious nature shows preferences in its modes of expression*. Here, too, the differences found in each soul evidently have much in common, for *these religious expressions fall into types which roughly correspond with types of sects*. The next inquiry must be concerning the great types into which human nature may be divided, not by the common sense of the average man, but by the careful study of the scientist.

It is a very striking fact that from Hippocrates and Galen to Kant and Wundt, the same classification of human nature has held sway. Through all these centuries the classification of Hippocrates into Choleric, Melancholic, Sanguine and Phlegmatic has seemed descriptive of the various kinds of human temperaments. Hippocrates found his explanation of these four temperaments in the presence of various properties in the system. Too great a proportion of yellow bile gives rise to a Choleric temperament, while black bile induces the Melancholic; so, too, the blood is responsible for the Sanguine and the phlegm for the Phlegmatic. Galen found the same four types of nature among his fellow-men, but sought to explain it upon other conditions, namely; the presence of heat, cold, dryness and moisture. Evidently, these ancient savants observed the kinds of temperament they encountered and then sought to find physical bases for them. Later philosophers sought to find the expanation of various temperaments in various organs of the body; some thought the thorax, the abdomen or the brains were the seats of various temperaments. Others tried to explain differences in temperament by the nervous system. Henle maintained that the sensor and motor nervous systems vary in tonicity, and that these variations account for differences in temperament. No less an authority than Wundt, the Nestor of modern experimental psychology, following Henle's cue, seeks to explain Hippocrates' four temperaments in terms of the quickness, alertness, energy and strength of mental processes. So he finds the quick-strong give the Choleric; the quick-weak, the Sanguine; the slow-strong, the Melancholic; the slow-weak, the Phlegmatic.* M. Fouillée finds the explanation of temperament in the processes which maintain life. These processes are the building up, anabolic,

* G. T. Ladd: "Outlines of Physical Psychology," 1893, p. 456.

and the tearing down, catabolic. These, he maintains, act something as the centrifugal and centripetal forces in mechanics. They act and react together; when the one set, the disintegrative, is active in greater proportion than the other set, the integrative, the result is a temperament of a characteristic kind. In this way he would account for the forceful, aggressive, expansive types and the quiet, retiring, placid types.* Fouillée sees in the activity of the male and the passivity of the female a corroboration of his theory.

Recent studies in physiology point out the influence of certain bodies, whose functions have long been mysteries, upon the temperament. The *thyroid body,* the soft, vascular body composed largely of blood-vessels, situated in the neck, fastened to the larynx, has a most potent influence upon an individual's entire life. When affected it may reduce one to an apathy which amounts almost to imbecility, or it may arouse one to a maniacal excitement. Another little body, very insignificant in appearance, is situated in the brain and has appeared to be of no service whatever. This *pituitary body* is now thought to exercise an influence upon the whole physical organism. It has long been known that the distinctive organs of the male and the female have very profound influences upon temperament, and that their loss, or injury, may occasion changes, which in the male tend to develop certain feminine traits; and in the female tend to produce certain masculine traits, such as growth of hair on face, deepening of the voice, etc. The circulatory system carrying nutrition to the whole body, the respiratory system supplying oxygen to the blood, both greatly influence the conscious life. Of

* A. Fouillée: "Tempérament et caractère," pp. 3-13, 76-80.

course, we cannot say that the seat of a certain temperament is in heart or lungs, because depression follows upon the affection of these organs; or an exhilaration follows upon their stimulation.

"Again we know that certain diseases tend to produce specific changes of temperament, that phthisis often gives it a bright and hopeful turn, diabetes, a dissatisfied and cantankerous turn. It is clear that, in some such cases of profound alteration of temperament by bodily disorder, the effects are produced by means of the chemical products of metabolism, which, being thrown out of the disordered tissues into the blood and reaching the nervous system by way of the blood-stream, chemically modify its processes.

"It is probable that every organ in the body asserts in this indirect way some influence upon our mental life, and that temperament is in large measure the resultant of all these many contributory chemical influences. Most of the bodily organs probably coöperate in determining temperament in another way hardly less important. All of them are supplied with afferent nerves—nerves that constantly carry impulses up from the organs to the central nervous system. And all these impulses probably modify in some degree the general working of the nervous system and play some part in determining the 'coenæsthesia,' the obscure background of consciousness on which the general tone of our mental life chiefly depends." *

It is evident that physiology cannot supply us with types of temperament. Its problems are so complicated, the factors entering into them are so numerous and

* Wm. McDougall: "An Introduction to Social Psychology," p. 119.

their analysis so intricate, that we cannot hope to find in the medical sciences of to-day any thorough-going explanations of types of human nature. Undoubtedly, the physical affects the spiritual in many ways, and could we understand these physical factors thoroughly, we might be in a position to classify all human beings according to their physical traits. To-day, however, it is impossible.

A much more promising line of approach is that furnished by the psychologist. He does not endeavour to connect consciousness and its physical seating, but studies the phenomena of consciousness alone. To the psychologist there are, also, several types of character and disposition. He makes his study from observations of temperaments themselves. One very interesting analysis of human nature is that of Malapert.* He finds the following factors in human nature, and their prominence causes these varieties. He finds that the emotions, the intellect, the will and actions furnish centres around which we may group various traits and class them as types of temperaments. Each of these central factors he studies carefully and finds that they represent a type of nature which may be divided into subtypes. The *Impressionable* type varies from the Apathetic to the Passionate and includes people incapable of strong lively impressions, and people with lively sensitivity but superficial, also, people with profound emotions which affect their entire being; and, also, the sentimental; and the irritable. Here is a varied assortment of kinds of impressionable, emotional folk. Somewhere in these lists we find a place for everyone whom we have considered of the emotional

* P. Malapert: "Las éléments du caractère."

type. Among those in whom *Intellect* is a predominant trait, Malapert finds the Analytic,—the doubter, the sceptic; the Critical type from which comes the connoisseur; the Conservative type, which includes the practical, the precise, the positive man who is also afraid of progress; the Speculative type which is constructive and given to large generalizations. Among those in whom *Volition* is a prominent characteristic, we find a series of classes ranging from the individual in whom the absence of will-power is striking, to those in whom it is ever active, from pathological cases to the great masters of achievements. In the *Action type* the range is from the indolent, the inert through the slow, heavy, dull, to the excitable, capricious and impulsive. Though this study is very suggestive, it is evident that some of these classes overlap to such an extent that they almost coincide. This makes it difficult to class anyone with any assurance. A simpler classification is needed.

Such a classification is afforded in part by Professor Giddings.

"Descriptive sociology has arrived at a stage at which it seems necessary to attempt to make a distribution of the population of any nation or community into psychological classes. We know, for example, that in the population of the United States are some tens of thousands of instinctive, animal-like creatures, passionate and violent; that thousands of others are imaginative, weakly but persistently emotional, and easily influenced by suggestion; that yet others are more or less fanatical, speculative, devoted to 'causes,' 'reforms' and so on, without end; and that, finally, some are critical, calculating, inductive, scientific. We know, further, that concerted volition of every description takes its character from the proportions in which these different psychological classes are combined. One combination makes the mob or the lynching party, another combination makes the deliberative assembly; one combination makes one sort of political policy and scheme of legislation, another combination makes a different policy and a different legislation. Great masses of statistics will acquire significance if the distribution of a population into psychological classes can be made. If the distribution is impossible, the statistics must remain meaningless.

"The analysis of mental phenomena into motor, affective (or emotional) and intellective aspects, suggests a threefold grouping." *

This threefold grouping Professor Giddings does not follow closely, but amplifies it into the ancient fourfold classification. It seems to me, however, that the three fundamental modes of mental phenomena furnish us an ample basis for a classification. All that appear in more elaborate tabulations may be entered under one of these heads.

Though we cannot find a physical basis for this classification of types of human nature, there is at least a suggestive analogy to be noted. The nervous system is, of course, one great system. However, its functions vary. There is the *sensory nervous system,* which conveys impressions to the brain. There is the *central nervous system,* the brain, which receives these impressions, retains them, combines them and then uses them in sending out impulses to the *motor nervous system,* which directs movements. It is easy to imagine

* *Psychol. Rev., 8,* p. 338.

that these three sets of processes will not operate in just the same way among all people. Certain bodily conditions may affect the sensory system so that one person is receiving a larger proportion of impressions, or sensations, or emotions than another; or the sensory system itself may be more susceptible to impression in one man than in another. Again, one central system, the clearing-house of impressions, may have greater retention, better coördination than another. While a third gives expression to his thoughts or his feelings more quickly, more easily than his fellows. So it is possible to imagine differences in the whole organism operating to influence these three portions of the nervous system; and the activities of these three systems in turn give rise to the Affective, the Intellectual, and the Motor types. However it may be with the physical bases of these types matters little; the important thing is that, in this tripartite arrangement of functions, we have a classification of human nature which is adequate.

Of course, these types do, in some measure, run into each other. Nevertheless, we have three large centers of native characteristics; their fringes blend, but the centres are distinct. To illustrate what is meant, let us consider several periods of human life. In the earliest years the motor factors are in greatest prominence. The child acts he knows not why. Dispositions wrought into the fibre of his being from countless generations of ancestors, express themselves independently of his control. He closes his hand when his palm is touched; he raises whatever he grasps to his mouth; he sucks everything suckable; he is a bundle of instincts. The first great business in life during the early years is to manage the body in relation to its surroundings, and this management is instinctive in great measure. It is the instinctive impulse to move the limbs which results in standing erect and in walking. There is the impulse to exercise which results in play. The hunting instinct in boys soon appears, and the fighting instinct to defend themselves, or what they may claim as their own. So, too, the maternal instinct in little girls to cherish and protect asserts itself very early. These little folk do a great many things which they are prompted to do without their giving the least deliberation to their behaviour. Under the heading of "Growth in Motor Power and Function," Stanley Hall describes this same sort of life as it appears in the early ages of the race.*

"For unnumbered generations primitive man in the nomad age wandered, made, perhaps, annual migrations, and bore heavy burdens, while we ride relatively unencumbered. He tilled the reluctant soil, digging with rude implements where we use machines of many man-power. In the stone, iron and bronze age, he shaped stone and metals, and wrought with infinite pains and effort, products that we buy without even knowledge of the processes by which they are made. As hunter he followed game, and when found, he chased, fought and overcame it in a struggle perhaps desperate, while we shoot it at a distance with little risk or effort. In warfare he fought hand to hand and eye to eye, while we kill 'with as much black powder as can be put in a woman's thimble.' He caught and domesticated scores of species of wild animals and taught them to serve him; fished with patience and skill that compensated his crude tools, weapons, implements and tackle; danced to exhaustion in the service of his gods or in memory

* Adolesence, Vol. I, p. 167.

of his forebears, imitating every animal, rehearsing all his own activities in mimic form to the point of exhaustion, while we move through a few figures in closed spaces. He dressed hides, wove baskets which we cannot reproduce, and fabrics which we only poorly imitate by machinery, made pottery which set our fashions, played games that invigorated body and soul. His courtship was with feats of prowess and skill, and meant physical effort and endurance."

Among adult human beings in civilized countries, the motor type is not considered a very high type. He is apt to be largely determined in his course of conduct by unreasoning promptings, instinctive impulses, by habits which he has formed, and, as we shall see later, by auto-suggestion; he does not reason in a straight line, he guesses. He does not concentrate his attention upon a problem, but allows his attention to be diverted by external interests. He is often very active and aggressive.

As the individual matures, there are a number of physical changes which occur during the age of adolescence. Most prominent among these are developments which make for the expansion of the emotional nature. Various organs change in size relative to the entire organism. It is then that the distinctive traits of sex begin to appear. Likes and dislikes, sympathies and antipathies become very pronounced. During these years it is what one feels that actuates life. This is the great emotional period of life. We cannot say exactly when the motor type gives place to the emotional type, or in just what proportion the emotional nature dominates over the other nature. But, anyone can easily observe the dominance of emotional characteristics in youths.

Among adults these traits of earlier years persist in varying proportions. Some are more impulsive, instinctive in their conduct than others, some are more impressionable, emotional.

Another situation presents itself in maturity. Here we have to do with the adult who has "found himself." He is no longer impelled by promptings which he cannot understand, nor is he swayed by emotions over which he does not seek control. He is deliberative, meditative, acts after he has represented to his mind the possible outcome of his action. He is less given to activity and to feeling than he was in his earlier years, though the traits of the earlier periods have not by any means entirely disappeared. Every sane adult has passed the period of unreasoning impulse and of emotions. Reason asserts itself in every normal adult. The point to be noticed is, that these other elements appear in greater proportion in one class than in another. In brief, we may not only divide our fellow-beings according to age, but we may also divide them into three great groups in which the characteristics of the three periods of life assert themselves.

IX

ACTION TYPES

WE have already seen in the survey of the sects that the Experiential type is the largest. In this type the feelings lie at the bottom of the religious life. Indeed, we may say that the feelings lie at the bottom of all religious life, of every type; but in the Experiential type the feelings are not only the foundation but they are, also, a large part of the superstructure. We saw in the survey of religious types that the emotional type occurred the most frequently. So it is perfectly safe to say that the feelings are the most conspicuous feature in religion. Professor Starbuck* defines the part the feelings play in religion by showing the value of feelings in other phases of life. For example, it is to the feelings that we turn in our judgments of Wagner's music, or Raphael's painting. These finer feelings are better capable of making judgments than any intellectual reasoning, they guide us with more certainty. In the common walks of life the feelings are often called intuitions and not infrequently play important and valuable parts in selecting our friends, governing our course of conduct and shaping the destiny of our lives. Is it too much to say that in spite of the misleadings of the feelings their true leadings have accomplished great triumphs in civiliza-

* *Amer. Jour. of Relig., Psychol. and Educ.*, *1*, pp. 168-186.

tion? May we not claim that the vigour and inspiration of life subside as the affective elements decrease? The feelings which represent the historic consciousness of the Christian church have stood as beacon lights of civilization. Love, the central theme of Christianity, is the one great hope of our wayward race. By it the ideals of civilization may ultimately become real and permanent.

It is impossible, as has been frequently said, to draw boundary lines around the qualities of human nature. Emotion is a prominent quality, so is intelligence, so is instinct. These blend with one another as the colours of the spectrum blend together. There are qualities of which we may say, this is distinctively an emotion and this distinctively intellect. Emotion then shades off on one side into intelligence and on the other side into instinct. This chapter is devoted to those qualities of human nature which may be called *action* qualities; truly the feelings run through them, but the feelings are not the characteristic things about them. It is not easy to find a descriptive word for these qualities, but, as they all make for action *directly,* they may be termed qualities which indicate an Action type.

In trying to understand human nature the best point of departure is in a study of animal nature. Here the problem is simplified. The first duty of every living creature is to act so that its life may be preserved; Nature is concerned first of all with the behaviour of an animal. Long before any structures appear which would serve for the seats of emotion or intellect there are structures to govern the movements of the animal. These movements are the priceless heritage of generations, the structure passed from parent to progeny has been evolved to do certain things on certain occasions; the doing of these things we call instinctive actions. Every lover of animals is familiar with a host of such activities.

Professor James defines instinct as "the faculty of acting in such a way as to produce certain ends, without foresight of the ends, and without previous education in the performance." * This definition has been criticised by a number of biologists and the tendency, now, is to recognize not exactly a foresight, but a sort of shadowy anticipation of a general result.† And along with this anticipation there may be, also, very elementary motive factors. However that may be, the facts remain that in the animal series from the lowest order up to man there are inherited functions which operate in a *quasi* mechanical way. "No agreement has so far been reached, as regards either the definition of instinct, or its place in the hierarchy of human actions; but it seems safe to say that the instinctive movement, whatever else it may be, is always initiated by the release of an inherited disposition; that the distinctive consciousness resembles the impulsive but is richer in organic components; and that there is a very close connection between instinctive and emotive reactions." ‡ On the physiological side the instincts are closely related to the reflex actions. A reflex action is seen in such a simple thing as the striking of the nerve below the knee-cap and the resulting jerk of the member; or, in the flash of light which makes the eyes blink. It is the simplest sort of nervous reaction. If the head is removed from a

---

* "Principles of Psychology," Vol. II, p. 383.
† *Brit. Jour. of Psychol.*, 3, p. 227.
‡ E. B. Titchener: "A Text-book of Psychology," p. 462.

frog and a bit of acid touches his body he reaches up and brushes the acid off with a foot; if that foot be held, then he uses another. Reflex actions in human beings are such things as coughing, sneezing, smiling, swallowing. These acts are done in a mechanical way. It is a case of touch-and-go; pull the trigger and the nervous system does the rest. By sensible gradations we pass from these mechanical performances to more complex actions, which we see first in children; such as crouching or running in the presence of a strange person or object. I have seen a baby, not a year old, flinch when a towel was thrown across the room, it had never been struck with anything, had never been threatened, scolded or roughly handled; the flinching was the expression of its organism in the presence of a menace. Children exhibit many instinctive traits such as crying when they are in pain, or when they are hungry; or turning the head away in order to reject something that displeases them, or in order to avoid seeing a stranger, whose presence seems to inspire in them bashfulness. The early efforts to walk and to speak and, above all, to imitate, certainly run back in their heritage through many generations. As the child becomes older the instinct of self-preservation shows itself in a disposition to fight or, as has often been pointed out, in the hunting instinct of boys. Social instincts also grow up which make for friendships, gathering into groups or "gangs." Even curiosity and the disposition to display one's self or one's possessions, and the counter dispositions of modesty and reticence may go back to instinctive roots.

All these instinctive traits run through various types of human nature; but they undoubtedly bulk larger in some types than in others. "The human mind has certain innate or inherited tendencies, which are the essential springs or motive powers of all thought and action, whether individual or collective, and are the bases from which the character and will of individuals and of nations are gradually developed under the guidance of the intellectual faculties. These primary innate tendencies have different relative strengths in the native constitutions of the individuals of different races, and they are favoured or checked at very different degrees by the very different social circumstances of men in different stages of culture; but they are probably common to the men of every race and of every age." * Of course, among primitive people these modes of behaviour are much more conspicuous than among civilized men. Civilization imposes uniformity. It requires certain courses of conduct which are complex and have been evolved and established by the men of intellectual types.

Another sort of action-quality in human nature is Imitation. We have alluded to it as a form of instinct; and so, undoubtedly, it is in the early stages of life. Such responses as the smile an infant gives in return for a smile, or a blow in return for a blow, or the attempt to repeat what he has heard are probably instinctive. Another form of imitative action appears in its pathological aspect in hypnotism, where the subject acts upon the suggestion of the operator. It appears also when the attention is very much concentrated and inhibition lowered. When Webster spoke in Faneuil Hall so intense were his hearers that, with the swaying of the speaker's body, the hearers swayed too. An impassioned leader may so arouse his hearers and so ab-

* Wm. McDougall: "An Introduction to Social Psychology," p. 19.

ACTION TYPES

sorb their attention that they follow him without carrying on their customary mental habits. Imitation of some skilful pianist, or craftsman, or writer, which is deliberate and painstaking is a very different thing from imitation of the instinctive type. In the latter we find a characteristic quality of a certain class of people. It is a characteristic of those who find action easier than deliberation; they do not wish to think around a subject or to think their way through it, they simply want a certain result and they go as directly for it as they can. They find that it is much easier to accomplish their purpose by mechanically doing what they have seen others do than by attempting any original method. They imitate others in the way they earn a livelihood, in the way they conduct their lives, in the manner they dress, in the thoughts they entertain and even in the emotions which move them.

In this same type of nature may be found those who easily follow an instinct and mould it into a habit. Whatever proves successful they cling to and repeat. There is no intelligent direction of trials, the trial that happens to meet their requirements is good enough for them. They settle upon one way of doing things and never think of departing from it.

Because action is so much more congenial than deliberation such folk are very susceptible to suggestion. It is hard for them to originate ideas, and when they do originate them the ideas are often of such unreliable character that they do not inspire confidence. An idea which comes from without often appeals to them with more cogency than anything which arises in their own minds. With their touch-and-go nature the presence of an idea means its performance if possible. It is enough to suggest, they instinctively carry out the suggestion.

The prominence of these traits, which I have called "Action Traits," gives rise to a very familiar type of human nature. It comprises those who might be called the *psychologically* poor; their principal endowments being those which served humanity in its earlier stages of growth. The finer feelings and the intellectual capacities, which have led the human race into civilization by the control of these inherited propensities, are not dominant in this type. It is the class one encounters so often among "the masses"; not that the masses are comprised entirely of such a type, or that the poor are poor because of lack of higher endowments; for there are many in the greater mass of poor who are so because of injustices in the social order. But, among those who are natively poor and who under the most fortunate circumstances would not be able to avail themselves of their opportunities we find the type described.

A man chosen at random from this class will not be a skilled workman, he has left school for something more congenial after he obtained the rudiments of an education, and he has picked up such jobs as he could. He seldom becomes a master workman except where dexterity alone counts. He does not look ahead and plan, he lives for the present. He has learned his occupation by imitating others. If he succeeds in following a trade he does so by imitating others. He prefers outdoor occupations, and insists upon an occupation which calls for action. He is restive and impatient when obliged to live a sedentary life.

In his social life he finds his recreation in almost any amusement which does not call for intellectual effort.

A "problem play" has no attraction for him. He prefers the circus or a vaudeville. His reading must startle him sufficiently to hold his attention. He prefers yellow journalism above all else with its panorama of suicide, murder, divorce and sporting news. Music attracts him if it is lively and tuneful, but nothing approaching an opera appeals to him. Anything which makes for refinement he considers snobbish and unmanly, his attitude is very much like that of a boy towards a girl's interests. As for his inner life, it is ordered by no intellectual control, he does not keep his attention upon any problem very long, and never upon a problem which is not concrete. Abstract questions are as far beyond him as interstellar space. If he plans a house it is a very simple plan. Mathematics have nothing to do with it. His attention goes immediately to things tangible, or seen, or heard; it is not held by any tight train of thought. When he reasons he does so by presenting illustrations and examples, but he does not follow the thread of argument upon which the illustrations hang. He is willing to talk, and talk a great deal; but uses emphasis for argument. His philosophy of life is gathered from his surroundings. His own experience is perplexing, for he has acted as he has felt prompted, without plan or deliberation. When he succeeded he did not see just why it was that success came to him and when he failed he did not trace the line of cause and effect. The world is not one orderly sequence of cause and effect, but is as sporadic as his impulses, to him. So he finds certain days are the best ones on which to bet, and that he gets sick " only on a Wednesday," that it pays to carry a lucky stone, that every time he walks under a ladder, or opens an umbrella in the house, his wife gets sick. Men, in his judgment, are actuated by very direct and obvious motives. They are against him "trying to do him," or "he stands in with them." The judicial frame of mind is an eagle's flight above his imagination.

The religious life of such a type is in conformity with all the rest of his life. The ideas which underlie his religious belief have been taken from others. He accepts without criticism the theology of his church. He imitates others in religion as he does in his work. He goes to church as he has been taught to do, it is habit. At church he goes through the forms which everyone else goes through, without question. However, only a certain form of service appeals to him at all; it must be a form in which he can *do* something. A service composed largely of an address which appeals to the intelligence is intolerable to him, and it is impossible for him to gather inspiration for the week's work from the ideas imbibed from a sermon. Thinking is not his specialty, his whole life is action. If he can do something, then he participates in the service. Let him rise, sit, bow, kneel, cross himself, make audible responses, protect himself with holy water, and he can enter into the spirit of the service. A confessional where one confesses aloud in the presence of an objective being enables him to get some grip upon his moral nature; but he could not in the quiet of his room, alone, unassisted, lift his thoughts to God and maintain his attention in prayer.

The Roman Church evolved from the needs of this type of nature. When Christianity spread through Europe it had to adapt itself by taking on a number of the traits of the religions which it supplanted; certain festivals were retained, certain customs could not be entirely obliterated and many ideas had to be incorporated in this new religion. Man found in the saints substitutions for their deities. It is easy to think of a saint and to look to a saint, who is little higher than one's self, for help. A Catholic friend of mine recently told another friend if he would find a house to ask St. Anthony to help him, as St. Anthony had proven a help before in just such an emergency. The relations between man and the Unseen must be as simple as possible, there must be things to do which count in the unseen world. There should be days set apart for certain things, days when one should not eat certain things, weeks for special observations, beads which can be taken in the hand and counted as one communes with the Unseen. In short, there must be numerous ways in which the Unseen can be made real. For this type reality is found by doing something, not by reasoning.

Of course, the Church of Rome does not supply the only form of worship for this type, though its evolution has been in conformity with such demands. The usual Protestant form of worship, with the emphasis upon the sermon, probably cannot be used; but the Protestant ideals and purposes could certainly be adapted to the psychological demands of the so-called masses. Where such an adaptation has been attempted the results promise well. The Salvation Army with its marching, its music, its exhortation, its participation in speaking, and its numerous practical activities have enabled it to appeal to much the same class of people.

An excellent hint is given to the Protestant churches by the numerous fraternal orders which have grown up in the last few years; for in many of these organizations there is a religious life which consists very largely in *doing* something. Indeed, these orders have cut deeply into the church membership, and many complaints are heard in church circles concerning the competition of the fraternities. Why not follow such an excellent example and attract this type of individual by enabling them to express their religious life in action?

The institutional churches in many of the large cities have attempted to put into practice the principles mentioned. Many men have started their religious interest in discussions concerning labour and capital held in the men's meetings of such churches. It seems a far cry from the heated discussions of politics and economics to the quiet of the devotional hour, but when the type of man we are considering has formed a habit of going to some one meeting place he will go to meetings whose interest may be far removed from his own. So it is not uncommon to see a number of men in one of the popular evening services of the institutional churches who throughout their childhood and, perhaps, early manhood, never entered a church. The question one often hears from these men is, "Well, what can the Church do for me?" That sounds selfish; but we must remember that these men are hard pressed by the hard circumstances of life. When a genuine interest in their welfare is shown in a way that they can understand and a genuine friendship is shown similar to the friendships they do understand, their question is satisfactorily answered for them.

The Protestant churches have been trying to meet this difficult situation for a number of years. Many of them have laid such great emphasis on their social work that the devotional side of church life has suffered. The solution must be found not simply in attracting large numbers of people to the church building, but in inspiring these people with some sort of religious life. As a matter of history the Protestant Church has had largely to deal with a type different from that we are discussing. The followers of Luther were people who were attracted by the appeal to their conscience and intelligence. Calvin's followers were appealed to largely through the intelligence, and the same might be said of Zwingli's adherents. The history of Protestantism is full of advance inspired by thoughtful leaders and worked out by intelligent people. The issue at present is simply this: How can the Protestant churches with their heritage meet the needs of a type which has hitherto been so successfully reached by the Catholic Church? From the present study several things are obvious; the first is that the service itself should be adapted to this type; the second is that habits of church-going should be acquired early; the third, some social pressure should be exerted, the custom made popular and attractive so that Imitation may do its good work.

Under the heading, Action Types, another class of people should be considered, a class which occupies a very different position in the social scale from that which we have just studied. Instinct within, Imitation without, were largely responsible for the behaviour of the first type. In this second type instinct and imitation play a very small part while intelligence plays quite a prominent part. It is the type we are familiar with in many American business men, practical men, men of action, men who claim that they are men of achievement rather than men of reflection and deliberation. I group them in this chapter because action seems the most eminent of their traits.

They are doers, not thinkers, though, of course, it would be wrong to say they do not think their way to action. The emphasis, however, is upon action, accomplishment. Sentiment has no part to play in their life work. They are governed by rigid facts of life in a practical world. If, in the beginning of their active careers, they carried sentiment into their activities, they quickly learned it had no place and no purpose. Furthermore, they do not believe in too much deliberation. Results are what count with them. Think quickly and accurately and then act, is their motto. After all, it is not the thinking that counts, but the result of the action. Such a man recently told me that he wished he had never taken a college course, for the habit of weighing and balancing acquired in college work was a positive detriment in business. While he was weighing the merits of a course of conduct, someone else went ahead and did what he was thinking about. We are very fond of saying that it is the practical man who has reared the great cities, and covered the continent with roads and irrigated the wastes of arid soil, and, indeed, accomplished all the things about which America boasts. How often the thinking man is crowded aside by the distinctively practical man! It is a common experience for one man to make an important invention and a man of a distinctively different type to make the money out of the patent. One of the best informed, most widely read lawyers in Wall Street was drawing a salary of $1,200 a year, a few years ago; while one of the most energetic, but not most intelligent, lawyers was employing him and making large sums out of his employee's intelligence. It is, then, to the practical type that the average business man is tending. He may have a splen-

ACTION TYPES

did symmetrical nature. He may be a patron of art, lover of music and a devoutly religious man, and he may carry these finer feelings with him throughout life. Indeed, a number of the greatest captains of industry have been just such well-balanced men. However, it requires a splendid strength of character to maintain these traits and men not strongly endowed with them are very apt to lose them entirely, or to reserve only their finer feelings for their home and their children. If we take a typical example of this class of men we find a man who is rarely affected by any appeal to his emotions, who is never sentimental and who, from the constant exercise of faculties which deal with purely practical things, becomes rather mechanical in his thinking and acting. For years he has habituated himself to collecting facts, arranging them and acting on them without any guesswork and without taking any chances. It is a hard matter-of-fact world with which he deals and, though he may at times be disposed to yield to the promptings of his feelings, the demands of life quickly over-ride any such disposition.

The religion of such a type is characteristic. The emotional nature, which plays a central part in religion, plays little part in his life. He is impatient with anything that seeks to affect him through his feelings. The service of the average church has little in it to attract him. He does not believe in "talkers," he "doesn't trust them," the men he meets who talk a great deal accomplish a very little. He naturally looks down upon a professional preacher. The only sort of a sermon that appeals to him is a practical sermon, dealing with things he knows and handles. A great cathedral with its lofty columns and stained-glass windows does not inspire him to sit and think and pray. It bores him. The symbols seem foolish, the ritual seems trivial, the whole thing is stupid. Among these men one often hears such expressions as: "My religion is common honesty," or, "My creed is simply the laws of the land," or, "My religion consists in helping the fellow who is down." Religion for these men must be something which enters into their lives as they are lived in the practical hustle of every-day business. If they can see a man who deals honestly with his fellow-man and shows leniency to the unfortunate and abides by the law, they admire his religion. If they see a church which is raising the moral life of a community and reaching out to help all classes of people, they will be willing to assist it, and will occasionally attend the services.

There is no sect composed of such a type, predominately. This is exceedingly strange. Christ was distinctly practical. He gave the world no system of theology, though innumerable attempts have been made to fashion theology out of what He said and did. These attempts have given rise to innumerable sects. He did, however, give a very clear-cut and intelligible system of conduct. He who runs may read and understand what Christ would have him do; yet no sect has ever grown up upon Christ's system of conduct. Isolated actions of the Master have given rise to feet-washing sects, baptizing sects, fasting sects and what not. This seems unintelligible at first, but when we remember that the religious nature must have its taproots in emotion, an explanation presents itself why the religion which has accomplished our civilization has not yet given birth to a sect which does not seek first to satisfy the claims of the heart.

It would be hard, indeed, to form a church of this purely practical type. The best we may hope from it is to attract men to the church in their earlier years and to hold them by keeping their finer natures alive and by engaging them in practical ethical work among their fellows.

In this chapter on Action Types we may well consider two rather scattering types of individuals. Before we attempt to describe them it will be profitable to look into the psychology of action. It is commonly held among psychologists to-day that every thought tends to express itself in some form of action. This is not always obvious. Many actions are so minute that they escape observation entirely. The principle, however, is very familiar in a number of experiences. When the novice first attempts to ride a bicycle he discovers a strong disposition to steer into objects he wishes to avoid. When he thinks of the tree, or the ditch, or the wall he finds himself steering into it. A very pretty demonstration is given with the *automatograph*. It consists in letting the hand rest lightly upon a surface which moves easily with every minute movement of the hand. These movements are traced out upon a piece of smoked paper. When a story is read describing the movements of the hearer it will be found that he has unintentionally moved his hand in the direction his thought has followed. This, of course, is the explanation of *muscle-reading*. Another way in which thoughts tend to express themselves in actions is by a quickening of the heart, or of the breathing, or in the vaso-motor system. These may be studied in the psychological laboratories. When an action results immediately from a thought it is said to be an idio-motor action, i.e., the person acts immediately upon an impression. Many of our actions are idio-motor; for example, when walking and conversing with a friend, as an acquaintance passes, one automatically raises his hat. There is no thought in the action, there is simply the sight of a friend which touches off the automatic movement. As I sit discussing a question with a student, the wind blows the paper on my table, I move a paper-weight over to hold the paper down, I give no thought to the action at all, and a few minutes later could not tell whether I had made such a movement or not. All through life we find this idio-motor activity behaviour as an ever-present servant.

Very unlike this idio-motor activity is the long and careful deliberation which never results in any course of conduct. In this one reason is set over against another and the moment of acting is continuously postponed.

Now between these two extremes, the touch-and-go and the merely deliberative, we find many gradations. There are, however, two general types of behaviour: in the first there is a disposition to act before mature deliberation. Such persons are like the old-fashioned musket that occasionally went off before there was time to prime it—much less to aim it. They act first and think afterwards, if at all. They are impulsive; thought and action are close-coupled. People of this type speak their minds before their minds are well made up; they rise and speak at meetings before they have matured their thoughts. Nothing is so unpleasant to them as the suspense occasioned by weighing and balancing reasons, they become very impatient with waiting. They would far rather hazard an action than hold to their deliberations. Every church is apt to be afflicted with people of this description. They lead forlorn causes, start impossible movements, attempt the impracticable. However, those churches where there is something doing all the time afford a more attractive field for their talents.

A very different type is presented in that class which tends to think long and seriously, but never to act. To them an action means a commitment to some cause about which they cannot decide. Frequently when they do come to a decision it is after being spurred by some outward stimulus; or they may become weary of their irresolution and act in defiance of their disposition. Of such are the "well wishers" which are to be found in all churches, they wish everyone well, they wish everything well, they are willing to pray without ceasing; but they seldom make their influence felt by their conduct. To these people those denominations that lay great emphasis upon the thought-life and little emphasis upon practical life are most congenial.

There are, then, very diverse types to be classed under the head of Action Types. One class we find constituting a very large proportion of the greatest sect in the country. Another class we find constituting a very large proportion of the non-church goers. And the smaller classes we find scattered throughout all denominations, but tending to gravitate where their particular temperaments are most comfortable.

X

EXPERIENTIAL TYPES

THE term experiential is intended to describe all those religious events in life which make profound impressions (because of their intimate personal character) and which are invariably associated with the emotions. *To experience,* etymologically, is *to go through.* Everyone appreciates the significance of the expression " to go through " an ordeal or a trial. A religious experience which one goes through is something more than the quiet growth into the religious life from a non-religious life, such as many excellent Christians have had. In church circles a religious experience implies a period during which one's nature is aroused in a characteristic way. The deliberate argument which a man may quietly and calmly hold with himself and which may lead him to change his whole course of conduct is not a religious experience. The stillness of a starlight night which quiets the mind and arouses the feelings of wonder and reverence can so impress a man that his whole life is guided thereafter by what he believes are God's purposes instead of selfish ones. That would be a religious experience. This is not the place to compare the relative worth of the emotional and intellectual influences which operate to arouse the spiritual nature. All that we need to do here is to note that the religious experience is associated with the feelings and that it is impossible without them. Indeed, any profound experience is impossible without them.

It is a very true truism that "no one lives his whole life above his collar"! There is no such thing as a "thinking machine" outside of fiction. Hard-headed people may be contrasted with soft-hearted people. Cold-blooded logicians may be the antitheses of high-spirited artists. Nevertheless, be the logician's head ever so hard and his blood ever so frigid, he is not completely devoid of feeling. Perhaps his feelings may be thinned out and attenuated in the estimation of more emotional natures, but some "feeling" remains. Such "feelings" may evidence themselves in the so-called "intellectual sentiments"; that is, in the pleasure derived from doing intellectual work, in appreciating the unity and balance of a problem, in the satisfaction of intellectual triumphs attained. When all emotion is gone life has gone. It is the time-honoured custom of comparing emotion and intelligence, of setting one over against the other, of accentuating the absence of one and the presence of the other, which has led to a popular confusion and to the fallacy that some people are *entirely* feelingless. Certainly, there are people in whom some of the feelings and sentiments, which are proper to wholesome natural lives, are absent. Still, that is a distinctly different thing from a life insensible to any affective influences.

When anyone "takes stock" of life and raises the old question whether it is worth living or not, the results of his meditations are always set down in terms of feeling! For what are happiness, contentment, the satisfaction of achievement, but feeling? Life may have innumerable hours which are colourless and insipid;

these we ignore. It is the moment of pain, of grief or of delight which rises up and is counted in our computation. Whether the Heaven of the Christian with its appeal to the best things in human nature, or the Heaven of the Moslem, with its appeal to the sensuous nature, stands before the mind as the "summum bonum" of all existence, the appeal is to the feelings. Many systems of philosophy and ethics unravel into an appeal to man's desire for happiness; which, psychologically interpreted, means an appeal to the emotions. All of which spells the character of life in terms of emotion.

Now, this presence and permeation of the emotional nature in one's life of thought and action does not seem to the average man an actuality. To the unsophisticated the routine of life runs its even course without much stir of the feelings. Only when an incident calls up anger, fear, patriotic fervour, gratitude, amusement or some other unusual excitement, does he realize he is an emotional creature. But, in reality, the train of his thoughts is constantly directed by feeling. If he pauses to consider them it is obvious that he does not think of his future grave, of his wife's death, or his children's possible dishonour and a myriad of similar sinister things for the simple reason that he does not like to. It is a matter of feeling. This is much more apparent in the twists and turns of a conversation. Here "the things that interest" him are taken up and talked over; which are also matters of taste, of feeling. When he has to think about or discuss uncongenial subjects he is fully aware of the feeling of aversion.

So feelings of all sorts run through everyone's life. They are not the same with all people, nor are they the same throughout life for any one person. The experiences of life take their shape and are largely determined by the amount of feeling and the kind of feeling with which a man is natively endowed. Before trying to understand the different kinds of religious experiences, it is necessary to understand some of the characteristics of man's emotional nature.

An interesting classification of the emotions appears in a recent work in psychology.*

"A persistent feeling, although not unduly strong, may yet be properly characterized as an emotion. . . . In this case we experience a mood. It is a continued feeling of pleasantness or unpleasantness, or restlessness or quiescence. It colours the whole of our consciousness, cognitive as well as affective, for a period of time. We have times of depression when no good fortune counts for much and when any bad luck casts us into the depths of despondency. And again we have periods of cheerfulness when even a serious misfortune seems trivial. These moods are characteristic of what is called the temperament. There are three readily distinguishable grades of intensity in emotion; moods, ordinary emotions and passions. A passion is the opposite of a mood. Unlike the latter it is extremely intense and also short-lived. Because of its great intensity it cannot last long. Indicative of the four grades of emotion which we habitually distinguish in speech are the following affective terms:

Mood	Weak Emotion	Strong Emotion	Passion
Wonder	Surprise	Astonishment	Amazement
Irritation	Aversion	Anger	Rage
Kindliness	Friendliness	Liking	Love
Chagrin	Mortification	Resentment	Exasperation

*R. M. Yerkes: "An Introduction to Psychology," pp. 182, 183.

"In general it may be said that the stronger or more intense the feeling which breaks in upon the unemotional consciousness the more numerous, vivid and intense the bodily sensations which it arouses and the stronger the emotion which is experienced. Those persons who are prone to violent emotions pass into them quickly and as quickly emerge from them. They lose their tempers almost instantly upon provocation, fly into a rage for a moment or so, and emerge from it almost before the person who has been the cause of the emotion has got well started toward an emotion of resentment. Passionate individuals are wont to be surprised because after they have recovered from their anger toward a person that person is likely to be at the height of his emotional experience and cannot be placated. This is an important individual difference.

"As there are eye-minded, ear-minded and touch-minded individuals among us, so also are there moody, even-tempered and passionate persons."

As in temperament, the emotional nature has been assigned to different physical causes. Professor James insisted upon the importance of the physical in its relation to the emotions. "If we fancy some strong emotion, and then try to abstract from our consciousness of it all the feelings of its bodily symptoms, we find we have nothing left behind, no mind-stuff out of which the emotion can be constituted and that a cold and neutral state of intellectual perception is all that remains. . . . Every one of the bodily changes, whatsoever it be, is felt acutely or obscurely the moment it occurs. . . . What kind of emotion of fear would be left if the feeling neither of quickened heart-beats, nor of shallow breathing, neither of trembling lips, nor of weakened limbs, neither of goose-flesh nor of visceral stirring, were present, it is quite impossible for me to think. Can one fancy the state of rage and picture no ebullition in the chest, no flushing of the face, no dilation of the nostrils, no clenching of the teeth, no impulse to vigorous action, but in their stead limp muscles, calm breathing, and a placid face? . . . Each emotion is the resultant of a sum of elements, and each element is caused by a physical process of a sort already well known." *

It is impossible to say exactly what physiological setting underlies different emotional characteristics. Nevertheless, it is undoubtedly true that many differences in the emotional nature of people may be traced to physical differences. The first great division into types which presents itself in this study is the division of the sexes. The physical differences here are of a very fundamental character. They run back from the human species into the lower orders of animal life. In the simpler forms of life the male is more active than the female, he does not live so long, he does not retain his energy, but dispenses it rapidly. With him there is undoubtedly more chemical action and higher temperature. The primary purpose of life for the female is to conceive, bring forth and nourish her progeny. She is usually larger than the male, reserving her energy for her offspring. A striking example is furnished by the cochineal. The female spends her life largely in nourishing her young. She has no wings, is immobile, is twice as large as the male, who is very active, with long white wings. Even after life is over her dead body serves as a protection

* Wm. James: "The Principles of Psychology," Vol. II, pp. 451, 452.

to her eggs until they are hatched. Throughout the animal series the same general principle holds true. The male is active and combative and changes in characteristics. The female is quite passive and conserves in herself the true type of the species. Fouillée calls attention to the fact that among human beings the lung capacity of women is about 2,500 cubic centimetres, that of man is about 3,700. So the absorbing of oxygen and elimination of carbonic acid are less active processes in women; the blood contains less hemoglobin and is poorer in albumen; the arterial pressure also is less. All these are signs, according to Fouillée, of less chemical activity in the female and less expenditure of energy. The nervous system of women, he believes, makes them susceptible to disorders rare among men, such as hysteria and "les névroses." Inasmuch as the visceral organs which take care of the nutrition of the future race are highly developed in women, the nervous system controlling the viscera is more developed, and there are more ganglia controlling "la vie végétative et sensitive." The feminine nature gives a physical reaction to emotions much more easily than it does in the masculine; witness, the blushing and the pallor and the innumerable shades of pink, of which the heroine in any modern novel is capable.

These physical distinctions run out into the realms of temperament, emotion and thought. The gallant Fouillée * admits that women have not a number of the traits which distinguish men but insists that the traits she does possess are of just as high and fine a character. Miss Thompson sums up the biological distinction between the sexes as follows: " The female represents the

* "Tempérament et caractère," pp. 241-246.

conservation of the species—the preservation of past gains made by the race. Her characteristics are continuity, patience and stability. Her mental life is dominated by integration. She is skilled in particular ideas and in the application of generalizations already obtained, but not in abstraction or the formation of new concepts. Since woman is receptive, she possesses keener senses and more intense reflexes than man. Her tendency to accumulate nutrition brings about a greater development of the viscera, and, since emotions are reflex waves from the viscera, woman is more emotional than man. The male, on the other hand, represents the introduction of new elements. Males are more variable than females throughout the animal kingdom. Everywhere we find the male sex adventurous and inventive. Its variety of ideas and sentiments is greater. Its activities are characterized everywhere by impulsiveness and intensity, rather than by patience and continuity. Men are more capable of intense and prolonged concentration of attention than women. They are less influenced by feeling than women. They have greater powers of abstraction and generalization.

"It is evident that, on the surface at least, the results at which we have arrived accord very well with this theory. Men did prove in our experiments to have better-developed motor ability and more ingenuity. Women did have somewhat keener senses and better memory. The assertion that the influence of emotion is greater in the life of women found no confirmation. Their greater tendency toward religious faith, however, and the greater number of superstitions among them, point toward their conservative nature—their function of preserving established beliefs and institutions." *

Undoubtedly women feel more and use their feelings more than do men, i.e., the feelings enter into her life's preference and decisions. I am acquainted with a young lady who remembers and associates events in the past by her feelings. For example, she will remember the theatre to which she went last evening by the feeling she had when approaching that particular theatre, which is in a downtown, noisy, dirty section; the play she will remember, first, by recalling how she enjoyed it, and, then, she will recall the details of the acts and the scenes. With the average man the recollection of the theatre would come to mind by some sort of a vague visual image of the playhouse; the play itself would occur to mind in terms of the footlights, curtains, costumes, actors and music. With this young lady the play of the feelings is very important in helping her to remember acquaintances. She does not remember the face or the voice, but she does remember the feeling of liking or disliking; after getting the same feeling, then the thought of the name presents itself. Perhaps this is rather an unusual case, perhaps this young woman is not typical; nevertheless it cannot be doubted that the feelings do enter into the everyday life of women much more than of men. Women have more finesse, tact, address; they do not reason from detail to detail, but reach their conclusions with a hop, skip and a jump. They cannot sustain the strain of concentrated attention as long as men can, but on the other hand, their sensibilities and, possibly, their quickness of association are greater.

* H. B. Thompson: "Psychological Norms in Men and Women," pp. 172-173.

These obvious traits and differences of nature should show themselves in the religious nature of the two sexes. Starbuck* points out that both boys and girls are converted to the religious life most frequently at about sixteen years of age, but almost as large a number of girls are converted at thirteen. Starbuck believes that the spiritual and physical aspects of development in individual instances tend to supplement each other. The girl develops earlier than the boy. In regard to the motives which lead the youths to the religious life, Starbuck finds that altruistic motives actuate the female more than the male, and that social pressure, urging, example and imitation affect the female more than the male. He finds that in the experiences which precede conversion such as the sense of sin, desire for a better life, depression, anxiety, doubt, etc., the differences seem to indicate that feeling plays a greater part in the religious life of the females, while the males are controlled more by intellection and volition.

"These results may be summarized and exhibited as follows:

Men.	Women.
Intellect more prominent; hence, more theoretical doubts.	Sensibility more prominent; hence, more doubts of personal status.
Emotion focused on definite objects and at definite periods; hence, more turbulence.	Emotion more constant, more diffused, more gentle.
Less suggestible, resist more, have more intense struggle, and less fulfilment of expectation. Attain more in solitude.	More suggestible; hence, yield more readily to ordinary influences. Attain less in solitude; have less intense struggle, and more fulfilment of expectation."

* E. D. Starbuck: "The Psychology of Religion."

Starbuck thinks that conversion for males is a more violent incident than for females; the man prepares for it longer, weighs the possibilities, resists the forces which oppose his will, and when they become irresistible the change is cataclysmic. In keeping with this it is a significant fact that girls first awaken most frequently on the emotional side and less often to the new insight into truth. The boys, on the contrary, have the emotional awakening less frequently, but organize their spiritual world more often as a moral one. In those unhappy years when one is trying to reconstruct his faith, the tendency among men is more often toward reshaping their rational conceptions of religion, while in women the reconstruction is rather in the inner life and experience.

Coe[*] says, "Granted that this generalization is correct, what religious differences should we expect to find between the sexes? We should expect that women brought up under continuous religious incitement and suggestion would exhibit greater continuity in religious feeling and less tendency to pass through religious crises. And this is, in fact, what we appear to discover. With men religion tends more to focus itself into intense crises. Women yield sooner and show more placid progress, while men pass through more definite periods of awakening.

"One of the very striking things about the religious autobiographies presented to me is that, while religion seems to be a sort of atmosphere in the life of women— something all-pervasive and easily taken for granted —with the men it is more sharply defined, brings greater

[*] G. A. Coe: "The Spiritual Life," p. 237.

struggles and tends more to climacteric periods. Men are more likely than women, it appears, to resist certain religious tendencies up to the point of explosion."

These different tendencies in the religious life of the sexes should show themselves in the denominations. We should expect the Christian religion, or any religion to appeal to men and to women differently. Obviously such large broad trends of nature as those we have just described must show themselves in the various organizations for worship. This is exactly what we do find. The Report of the Bureau of the Census for Religious Bodies, 1906, shows that women predominate in all the sects. This is so universal that it cannot possibly be a matter of chance. In different states the proportion of males and females in the population will vary, and in some parts of the country there will be more women in the churches than in other parts, but throughout the country as a whole the women predominate in all the churches. A number of influences make the statistics uncertain. Immigration brings more males to this country. Consequently many churches are recruited from abroad by males more than by females and this gives them the greater proportion of males than they would normally have. Of course this applies more to the Catholic Church than any other. In order to get a fair comparison of the way in which different denominations build up their congregations from the two sexes, I have taken a number of cities and several denominations and computed the per cent. of women in these different denominations for these same cities.

PER CENT. OF WOMEN MEMBERS

	Christian Science	Baptist	Unitarian	Methodist	Congregational	Episcopalian
Portland	—	65	58	67	70	69
Manchester	—	68	63	65	72	66
Boston	73	62	64	63	68	62
New York	71	64	55	64	63	60
Cleveland	69	62	61	61	62	60
Chicago	70	61	63	62	60	62
Detroit	69	64	—	63	61	65
Denver	73	63	56	62	64	59
San Francisco	70	—	72	56	63	66
St. Louis	71	59	—	61	65	64
Des Moines	—	63	—	63	65	64

Note.—In taking averages throw out highest and lowest figures for each column.

It seems at first sight that these tables would give a very good idea of the way in which the different denominations appeal to the different traits in the sexes; but a further study shows that there are so many influences operating that the natural trends of the sexes are almost obliterated; thus, in the same denomination there will be considerable differences in the proportion of women belonging to its churches in the same city. Social influences and economic conditions play a very important part and these do not yield to any accurate measurement. Nevertheless, in spite of all the cross currents from immigration and social conditions, the main stream of tendency should show a definite direction. Such a tendency certainly does appear in the differences of proportion for women in the Unitarian and the Christian Science churches. Thus 70 per cent. of the members in the Christian Science Church are women, while 60 per cent. in the Unitarian are women. This same proportion runs throughout the country. Certainly the Unitarian Church is the preeminently intellectual church in America. Harvard University is the great expression of its spirit and ideal. For many years it has appealed to the intellectual people of the most intellectual section of the country. Compare the utterances of Channing and those of Mrs. Eddy! What could be further apart? Channing's appeal is to straight thinking, clean-cut and definite. Mrs. Eddy appeals to those who wish above all else for health. This wish is a profound emotion, there is " will to believe "; the matter of detailed argument is insignificant with such people. They do not get any clean-cut, logical conceptions out of Mrs. Eddy's philosophy, if it may be called such; they do get a feeling that there is a profound argument going forward, which they do not understand, but with whose conclusion they are in hearty sympathy. Women find this sort of an appeal more cogent than do men.

It is the "argumentum ad feminam," and is stronger than the "argumentum ad hominem." One would expect the tenets and practices of the Christian Science churches to appeal to women more than to men, and this the statistics certainly prove beyond question.

It is not quite easy to say why the Congregational churches average 65 per cent. women, while the Methodist, Baptist and Episcopal average around 63 per cent. It is true the Congregational Church is strongest in New England, where women outnumber men more than in any other section in the country, but that does not seem a sufficient explanation. Perhaps the true reason lies in the character of the Congregational Church today. It is not a doctrinal church, it is no longer interested in questions of theology, its appeal to-day is to the religious life, to the religious experience, to *altruistic motives*. The emotional life of the denomination is sober, sane and uniform. These traits, and its well-known altruistic traits, probably account for the large proportion of women in it.

It is interesting to see that the Methodist Church, which insists upon a definite experience, a conversion, does not appeal to the emotional nature of women any more than do the exercises of the Episcopal Church, through which one grows easily and naturally into the church membership.

The most important truth which the statistics give us is the great truth that Christianity appeals to the finer things in human nature, and is responded to by that sex in whose nature the higher feelings play the greater part. Where Christianity has been distorted under the leadership of a woman it appeals much more to certain distinctively feminine traits. Among these feminine traits is suggestibility. By suggestibility is meant the strengthening of one idea or set of ideas at the expense of the idea, or ideas, which would naturally be in opposition; that is, the natural procedure of one's thinking is interfered with in such a manner that the balance of one idea over against another is destroyed and the balance is tipped in the favour of the one rather than the other. In hypnotism the mind is in an abnormal condition and one idea is strengthened at the expense of all others, and the subject carries out that one idea, ignoring all others. In a state of excitement one idea arises in mind and takes possession of the field of thought and the individual hastens to carry out this idea. Professor Münsterburg says:* "The readiness to accept sugges-

*H. Münsterberg: "Psychotherapy," p. 88.

tions is evidently quite different with different individuals. From the most credulous to the stubborn we have every degree of suggestibility, the one impressed by the suggestive power of any idea which is brought to his mind, the other always inclined to distrust and to look over to the opposite argument. Such a stubborn mind is, indeed, not only without inclination for suggestions, but it may develop even a negative suggestibility; whatever it receives awakens an instinctive impulse towards the opposite. Moreover, we are all in different degrees suggestible at different times and under various conditions. Emotions reënforce our readiness to accept suggestions. Hope and fear, love and jealousy, give to the impression and the idea a power to overwhelm the opposite idea, which otherwise might have influenced our deliberation."

The principle of suggestion which we find operating to induce health in Christian Science students is a principle which appears in other forms of the Christian church, so it will be well to tarry for a moment and to study suggestion in its relation to religion. In religion we have seen emotion play a very essential part and, also, emotion is the chief assistant of suggestion. Now, suggestion often acts in an unconscious manner; e.g., when we are walking in the business sections of Chicago we find ourselves hurrying along in true Chicago style, though there may be no reason for our hastening. Others hurry, so we hurry, and are surprised when we discover ourselves hurrying. In this instance the suggestion comes from those surrounding us and we are unconsciously acting out what is given us. Another form of suggestion, more difficult to understand, is that which we give ourselves and which works out some time after we are conscious of giving ourselves such a suggestion. I find that if I think about making certain thrusts and parries in fencing that, when I come to fence six hours or a day after going over the movements in my mind, I actually do better work in the bout. Perfectly honest men have thought about methods of getting rich quickly (which they would not practise) but after years of thinking such matters over some exceptional opportunity has been the means of starting many a man along the line which he had discussed with himself, but had never intended to pursue. " Out of the heart are the issues of life," saith the Scriptures. " Out of the thoughts which habitually occupy the mind comes the conduct of life," saith Psychology. There are some types which carry out into action what they have suggested to themselves much more easily than do other types. Professor Coe found a considerable difference between people who had striking religious conversions and those who failed to have such conversions, though they had expected them quite as much as those who had succeeded in having them. It would appear from his study that the suggestions arising in mind concerning the experience which one is to go through may actually be lived out by a certain type of nature. He found that women, whom we have seen are more suggestible than men, pass through the experience they expect more readily than do men. He also found among those who expected a certain transformation in conversion, and who experienced it, were individuals who had, at one time or another in life, experienced motor *automatisms*. They had heard voices speaking when all was quiet, they had seen flashes of light, had dreamed dreams and seen visions of an extraordinary character. Coe also believes that this sort of suggestibility renders a subject more easily hypnotized than is normally the case. We have, then, a type of nature which couples together emotionalism and suggestibility and which works toward a certain kind of religious experience. We have seen that there are churches which insist upon a definite transformation in life, a dying of the old self, a birth of a new self. Such churches would naturally be recruited from the type of people we have just described. The old-fashioned Methodist Church, such as may be found to-day in rural communities, was distinctly of this type. The city churches to-day look askance at revival methods which were considered the work of the Lord a generation ago. Indeed, a very large number, a constantly growing number, of religious leaders are working away from the idea that a definite, clean-cut transformation is the natural way to pass from the irreligious to the religious life. It is becoming more and more realized that religion is a perfectly natural thing and that a child should grow up into religious thoughts and feelings as he matures. This does not mean that the type of nature which can swing from one kind of life to another in a short time shall be ignored. Certainly, there is a place for revival work; surely, the rough, effective methods used by our fathers are not entirely useless to-day, though the attitude of the present age is against them. The forces of civilization are raising the general level of intelligence, the public school is levelling the whole population. The emotional upheavals which appeared, for example, in politics a score of years ago are not possible to-day. It is to be expected that the old revival method would also pass out with the coming of universal education and the emphasis upon the intellectual rather than the emotional.

Professor James, in speaking of the two types of religious nature, says,* " There is thus a conscious and voluntary way and an involuntary and unconscious way in which mental results may get accomplished, and we find both ways exemplified in the history of conversion, giving us two types which Starbuck calls the volitional type and the type by self-surrender, respectively. In the volitional type the regenerative change is usually gradual, and consists in the building up, piece by piece, of a new set of moral and spiritual habits." The self-surrender type is the type in which suggestion works unconsciously and one surrenders to it; it appears to develop subconsciously. " Emotional occasions, especially violent ones, are extremely potent in precipitating mental rearrangements. The sudden and explosive ways in which love, jealousy, guilt, fear, remorse or anger can seize upon one are known to everybody. Hope, happiness, security, resolve, emotions characteristic of conversion can be equally explosive. And emotions that come in this way seldom leave things as they found them" (op. cit., 19). There can be no question that there is a *conversion type* of Christian and that we find this trend in human nature expressing itself in a large group of sects.

Among primitive people, Davenport † found many traits which appear in those who succumb to the influence of Christian revivals. He thinks that the same mental and temperamental traits enter into the exer-

* William James: "The Varieties of Religious Experience," p. 206.
† F. M. Davenport: "Primitive Traits in Religious Revivals."

cises of primitive man and the conversions of the revival. In describing primitive man he says, " We may mention together a group of primitive characteristics, the chief of which is nervous instability with its inevitable accompaniments of remarkable imitativeness and suggestibility and great lack of inhibitive control" (p. 18). " Primitive man is led to action by impulse rather than by motives carefully reflected upon. His opinions are chiefly beliefs, that is they are products of imagination and emotion. And because there is so much emotion in his opinions, it carries him quickly into action. His will power, in any high sense, is relatively weak" (p. 21). Davenport calls attention to the appearance of the sensory and motor automatisms. The convulsions, hallucinations and visions, a whole group of reflex phenomena. These appear among the Indians in their ghost-dances, among the American negroes in their camp-meetings and in many of the revivals among the whites. The way in which the religious dance of the Indians spreads from tribe to tribe is very suggestive of the way in which the great revivals spread from place to place throughout Kentucky. Both are due to imitativeness, which rests upon suggestibility. In reading Davenport one cannot help being struck by the very numerous instances in which women figure prominently in these Indian dances, or negro meetings or great Christian revivals. It is an Indian girl who first succumbs to the influence of the religious dance. Almost every entry quoted from Wesley's Journal speaks of the influence of the Methodist religion of that day upon women.

It certainly is not too much to say that those strains in human nature which lead men and women to the religious experiences characterized often as sudden conversions, trances or visions are strains resulting from a nervous instability.

In the so-called Holiness movements which have appeared in recent years, and which have appealed to a class of people of little education, many of these traits which are described as characteristic of primitive people come forth. These same paroxysms, the same phenomena of hypnotic character are easily recognized. It is not at all unusual in these Holiness meetings to see the old-fashioned camp-meeting emotionalism, to hear a fervid brother, or sister, give utterances to a soul-shaking shriek, or to rise and start a march, while singing, up and down the aisles of the meeting-house. I have known an enthusiastic convert who had given up a dissipated life and had become "sanctified," to stand in the meeting, shout and sing, give way to his impulses and cry " all who want to go to Heaven, follow me "; then he led a parade around the meeting-hall. A calm, unexcitable nature is invariably considered, in these circles, as lacking in spirituality and as incapable of receiving spirituality or inspiration. Of course, among the negroes, not influenced by city life, many of the revival phenomena are still to be seen; though it is greatly to the credit of the negro people that, despite their native tendencies, they have so largely abandoned their old customs. Among the Methodist churches it is hard to distinguish a Methodist service from any other, so far have they grown away from the methods of the early part of the last century. Cities have a very great levelling influence, and have shaped the worship of the different denominations after one general pattern, which is congenial to the spirit of the age.

EXPERIENTIAL TYPES

After this recital of the objectionable features in the strongly emotional nature, it is but fair to cite some of the advantages of this same nature. Emotion is one of the first characteristics of youth. The buoyancy, the exhilaration of the years of adolescence are the outcome of natural emotion. What would we not give in the even, sober, routine of middle age for some of the riotous, uproarious enthusiasm of youth! Is not the dead-line of forty the place where life slips away from the inspirations of the emotional nature into the matter-of-fact disposition of the practical man? No one has expressed the worth of emotion better than Professor James.* "Where the character, as something distinguished from the intellect, is concerned, the causes of human diversity lie chiefly in our differing susceptibilities of emotional excitement, and in the different impulses and inhibitions which these bring in their train. Let me make this more clear.

"Speaking generally, our moral and practical attitude, at any given time, is always a resultant of two sets of forces within us, impulses pushing us one way and obstructions and inhibitions holding us back. 'Yes! yes!' say the impulses; 'No! no!' say the inhibitions. Few people who have not expressly reflected on the matter realize how constantly this factor of inhibition is upon us, how it contains and moulds us by its restrictive pressure almost as if we were fluids pent within the cavity of a jar. The influence is so incessant that it becomes subconscious. . . .

"So far I have spoken of temporary alterations produced by shifting excitements in the same person. But

* W. James: "The Varieties of Religious Experience," pp. 261, 265, 266.

the relatively fixed differences of character of different persons are explained in a precisely similar way. In a man with a liability to a special sort of emotion, whole ranges of inhibition habitually vanish, which in other men remain effective, and other sorts of inhibition take their place. When a person has an inborn genius for certain emotions, his life differs strangely from that of ordinary people, for none of their usual deterrents check him. Your mere aspirant to a type of character, on the contrary, only shows, when your natural lover, fighter or reformer, with whom the passion is a gift of nature, comes along, the hopeless inferiority of voluntary to instinctive action. He has deliberately to overcome his inhibitions; the genius with the inborn passion seems not to feel them at all; he is free of all that inner friction and nervous waste. To a Fox, a Garibaldi, a General Booth, a John Brown, a Louise Michel, a Bradlaugh, the obstacles omnipotent over those around them are as if non-existent. Could the rest of us so disregard them there might be many such heroes, for many have the wish to live for similar ideals, and only the adequate degree of inhibition-quenching fury is lacking.

"The difference between willing and merely wishing, between having ideals that are creative and ideals that are but pinings and regrets, thus depends solely either on the amount of steam-pressure chronically driving the character in the ideal direction, or on the amount of ideal excitement transiently acquired. Given a certain amount of love, indignation, generosity, magnanimity, admiration, loyalty or enthusiasm of self-surrender, the result is always the same. That whole raft of cowardly obstructions, which in tame persons and dull moods

EXPERIENTIAL TYPES

are sovereign impediments to action, sinks away at once. Our conventionality, our shyness, laziness and stinginess, our demands for precedent and permission, for guarantee and surety, our small suspicions, timidities, despairs, where are they now? Severed like cobwebs, broken like bubbles in the sun."

After all, the world to-day is a young man's world; men of seventy who are still in the heyday of success are invariably young men at heart. When the impelling power of the emotions ceases, there is no longer any steam to keep the machinery going. In no institution, or organization, is this more obvious than in the Church. The difference between a vigorous church and a supine, inert one, is enthusiasm. Surely it was the ardour of the followers of Wesley that inspired England, when the nation appeared to be listless and run down. The great achievements of the Elizabethan age were in the past. That nation seemed to be in the winter of its existence; with the uprising of Wesley's movement came new inspirations and new incentives which affected the whole social order. In the United States the Methodist Church swept from coast to coast, every city, village, crossroads and countryside possessed its enthusiastic churches. From one of the smallest churches during the Revolutionary period it quickly grew to the greatest. Whatever may be said of the extravagance of its revival methods, it remains true that it has achieved a wonderful success. Indeed, the excesses of the revivals are often overemphasized. Though some shocking things are recorded of the Kentucky revivals it must be acknowledged that these same revivals improved Kentucky most wonderfully.

In emotion a number of various types may be found.

It is not right to speak of emotion as though it were of but one quality, obviously there are different kinds of emotion.

Ribot * declares, "There exists an *Affective Type* as clear and as well-defined as the visual, the auditory and the motor types. It consists in the easy, complete and preponderant revivals of affective impressions. . . . There exists not only a general emotional type; it admits of varieties, and it is even probable that partial types are the most frequent. . . . I have not at present a sufficient supply of documents to enter on the study of the varieties of the affective type; but it is certain that they exist; that for some, a clear and frequent revival only takes place in the case of pleasurable impressions; in others, of gloomy or of erotic images. . . . Individual differences in the revivability of emotional states certainly play a great part in the constitution of different types of character. Moreover the existence of variations of the emotional type cuts short the question, acrimoniously debated by some writers, whether pains can be more easily remembered than pleasures. Optimists and pessimists have fought fiercely over this fantasmal problem; but it is a vain and factitious question so long as we suppose that it admits of but one solution. There is not and cannot be a general answer.

"Certain individuals revive joyful images with astonishing facility; sad memories when they arise are easily trodden down. I know an inveterate optimist, successful in all of his undertakings, who has much difficulty in picturing to himself the few reverses that he has

* Ribot, Thomas: "The Psychology of the Emotions," pp. 167, 169.

experienced. 'I remember joys much more easily than painful states,' is an answer I frequently meet with in my notes. On the other hand, there are many who say, 'I remember sorrows much more easily than pleasurable states.' In the course of my inquiries I have found that the latter are the most numerous; but I do not see my way to draw any conclusions from this fact. One says, 'I find it much easier to revive unpleasant feelings, whence my tendency to pessimism. Joyous impressions are evanescent. A painful recollection makes me sad at a joyful moment; a joyful recollection does not cheer me at a sad one.'"

In another chapter the two great trends in the causes which have given rise to the sects are found to lie in two distinct dispositions; the one looks forward hopefully, courageously, cheerfully to future improvement, the other looks backward dissatisfied with the present, seeing no good for the future, desiring to return to the past. Under these two dispositions lie differences in the emotional nature, the same differences which appear in the Radical and the Conservative. Every political body, every government knows these two types; one is the party of progress, for it the golden age lies ahead; the other is the party of precedent, for it wisdom is to be found among the Fathers, and only there. In this difference of the emotional nature we find the explanation of the austere Puritan and the cheery, wholesome optimist in the churches which spring up as our civilization sweeps westward. Compare the characters of Henry Ward Beecher and Jonathan Edwards! Contrast the popular, progressive, successful church with the doctrinal, unsocial church clinging to historic traditions. It is a far cry from the people who cannot endure an organ in their church service to the people whose evening service is a sacred concert. This contrast impressed me very forcibly when in a village in Bavaria. Being accustomed to the austerity of a New England town, the Sabbath among these people, reputed to be the happiest in Europe, was a revelation. To see the priest mingling among the people as they gathered in a great garden, laughing and talking and sipping their beer all in high good humour, carefree with a loving God above them and no thought of offending Him, was to me a startling, new idea of the relation of Church and people. Here, there was no repression, no need for repression; the simple, natural people were enjoying themselves in a wholesome way, not, perhaps, *impossible* to the New Englander; but certainly uncongenial to the Scotchman and his Kirk. No one can mingle among people of different racial temperament and expect the churches representing these types to be the same in America. No one, indeed, can study human nature and look upon the differences in church life as radical differences of religion. The sooner the churches realize that their differences are to be found in human nature and not in God, the sooner will Christ's ideal that we are all one in Him be realized.

The last feature of the emotional type is a most important one. It has been pointed out continually that thought and feeling are bound together. Thought influences feeling and feeling influences thought.

This intimate relation between feeling and thinking has been known to orators for ages. Often Reason cannot carry its point and Emotion is called in to do the work. Cicero did not satisfy himself with a recital of Catiline's treacherous performances. He aroused the emotions of his hearers with allusions to their protecting gods, their sacred city, the safety of their homes and lives, the lustre of their honour and good names. He played upon the whole keyboard of their feelings and in the rush and whirl of the excitement all counter-arguments were forgotten and the balance of judgment swept away. Warren Hastings declared that Burke's eloquence so touched the emotions that he forgot the truth of the situation in his sympathy with the orator. Very often the politician finds an old battle-flag a much more effective argument than economics and sociology.

Men do reach their conclusions with more than "mere reason," as a general rule. The seduction to think as they feel is too cogent and potent. Only the singularly honest and clear-minded avoid the temptation to follow the line of least resistance, and refuse to shape their convictions to their desires. Hosts of most estimable people declare of something "that is a horrible thing to believe, I couldn't believe that"; and they could not because their minds are in partnership with their feelings and their feelings take another course. This is proverbially true of our thoughts about our children, our near relatives and our best friends. Nothing can make the lover see the flagrant defects of his lady, or the famous virtues of his rival! Perhaps one reason for this is the concomitance of certain classes of thoughts with certain classes of emotions. Evil, dangerous, loathsome objects invariably call up emotions of disgust, fear, antipathy. Indeed, the quickness with which these emotions arise is often astonishing. I have found the feeling of aversion arise when a distorted face was displayed in a tachistoscope before the face was fully seen in its hideousness. The feeling of revulsion was an *accompaniment* of recognition and not *subsequent* to it. Such constant and natural association of feeling with thought may well cause the influence of feeling upon thought. If evil is associated with hatred and good with love, it is easy to see how an argument which calls up feelings of disgust and aversion will predispose the mind to a very different sort of conclusion than it would be apt to take if the course of argument brought forth sympathy, kindness and affection. Indeed, it may well be said that it is unnatural to be impervious to the "argumentum ad hominem."

A remarkable sidelight is thrown upon the subject by studies in abnormal psychology. The "insistent idea" which takes a stronger and stronger hold upon the mind until it has deranged the equilibrium, is started in its course by some accompanying emotion. In time the emotion which racked the soul is forgotten, but the idea which was engendered in the heat of the moment is clear and prominent. May not this explain many of the ideas which endure so stubbornly? They were made part of our beliefs during some great emotional experience and the impress made upon the mind in those moments of plastic suggestibility has hardened into a permanent possession. This would explain why some clear-minded men still cling to old illusions though they acknowledge that they cannot defend them. I know an old soldier who fought for a wrong cause. In the fervour of youth and high ardour he enlisted. To this day he is blind to the reason of his old foes.

For many people the catechism which they learn in their early youth has become a part of their philosophy. It was taken into their lives surrounded with the most precious influences; the memory of the long evenings in which it was memorized, is a memory which treasures the love of an affectionate mother and a host of tender associations. Into one's life its precepts enter bound up with the most enduring and endearing affections, and when in later years the things it taught are brought into question, it is not an intellectual matter, but seems rather to be a matter which concerns itself with one's loyalty to one's dearest connections. No man can receive his religious instruction from those whom he has loved and admired, and then in a quiet, dispassionate way change his convictions. Many students come to our universities with a philosophy, or rather a theology, which is not in keeping with the thought of their times; often they experience several years of reconstruction in their thinking. So intimately bound up is one truth with another in their training that they are often tempted to throw over all their religious convictions when one of them is assailed. Not infrequently a man of deep feeling and strongly loyal nature will cling to his youthful teaching in spite of all. He cannot let it go, it is too dear to him. The responsibility for his predicament lies with his church and his home; they should have acquainted themselves with the thoughts of the day, and though they were out of sympathy with them, they should have sought to build up a religious faith which would not be shaken when it came in contact with the intellectual movements of the present.

In this principle of relation between thought and feeling lies the explanation of many archaic beliefs. Long ago impartial thinking men gave up a number of the tenets which grew out of the Reformation. It is wicked to teach youths doctrines which they cannot intelligently hold when they mature. Nothing is more distasteful to a young man than that which savours of hypocrisy. A church which argues that one must believe certain things because they are a part of the church tradition and doctrine is making an appeal to the emotions, not to the intelligence. When a teaching of science is attacked by the Church, as it often is, with the argument that if science is right then we must surrender the cherished beliefs of our fathers, it is an argument which appeals only to those who hold to their beliefs because they are cherished. There are many people who hold to their beliefs for no other reason. They frankly confess that they cannot believe this, or they cannot believe that, not because the beliefs are unintelligible, or do not conform with facts, but because they conflict with the believer's own likes and dislikes. Open-mindedness is as much a matter of the heart as of the head. In the South, among people who are famously warm-hearted, kindly, sociable, hospitable, the old conceptions hold sway much more effectively than in New England. In the South a quotation from the Bible closes an argument; in the North such a quotation starts an argument. To be broad-minded and to be willing to shape one's convictions to one's intelligence, requires more than mental vigour; it requires a courage possessed only by the sturdiest hearts. Surely, the world should deal kindly with the bigot who clings to his dogma because it became his possession along with many of the noble things which have entered his life. The best things of the doctrinaire are his loyalty and his devotion; these should not be forgotten when he is censured for obstructing the progress of Christianity.

Unquestionably, there is a place for the prejudice of the doctrinaire in the changing thought of to-day. It is as great an error to change with every changing wind of doctrine as it is to be interred in the grip of tradition. The unstable mind is one which has no anchorage in any strong emotion. The present age calls for men of deep feeling who have won their convictions in intellectual battles, and who do not easily surrender them, but who are willing at any time to enter the battle again and are willing to change their convictions not only for their own good but for the good of coming generations.

XI

INTELLECTUAL TYPES

IT is commonly believed that the differences between men in matters of intelligence are simply the differences between the bright and the stupid. There is a word for "fool" in every language. Psychology supplements such obvious distinctions with a number of more refined discriminations. The laboratories have been busy for a generation seeking out inconspicuous mental differences in men. When such differences are descried everyone recognizes them and wonders why they have not been noticed before. Some of the results of this work bear directly upon the differences in religious thinking. In this chapter several of the characteristics of different mental types are presented.

The most interesting feature of all the thinking processes is the *attention*. It is the focal point into which the rays of conscious life gather. Constantly shifting its position with reference to the whole field of consciousness, it is always the "clearest area" of consciousness. Its strength is the strength of the mind. Its weakness is anarchy. When the mind cannot gather itself for vigorous application, independent of distraction, and cannot persist in its own course, then the soul becomes a derelict, tossed in every direction by all the passing fancies and feelings.

INTELLECTUAL TYPES

Two great Types of attention are easily recognized; the Voluntary and the Involuntary. Every mind is party to both. In voluntary attention the thoughts are self-guided and independent of external distraction; one consideration suggests another according to the principles of mental life. In involuntary attention the thoughts are directed from impressions without, or drift as in a reverie. The former is more easily occupied with ideal, or intellectual objects, the latter is more readily given to objects of sense. With education the attention becomes better adapted to grasp and master the ideal. For this reason the pictures and diagrams of the youth's text-book give place to the close-knit thoughts of the university texts, and the symbols and rites of a religious organization become shallow and unserviceable to the mind which can keep its hold upon ideal things without the aid of material means.

A natural division appears between those religious organizations which seek to reach the cultured and those that attract the uneducated. Certainly, their work would be more efficient if the natural disposition of the attention were recognized in the two orders of minds. There are many bare, plain churches where the strong-headed sons of the Puritans can find spiritual inspiration in the words of some clear-minded preacher, but where the labourer, who seldom controls his attention for any length of time, and whose education has never demanded concentration of thought, would find the service unprofitable and dispiriting. The thinker, with the habits of years in directing a mind whose thoughts have been his life, finds the obvious symbolism and the simple truths of the ritualistic churches stupid. That is, such is the *natural tendency*, and such is *usually* the case, though many things enter into men's religious preferences; and occasionally the most cultivated and alert minds find their spiritual comfort in repeating a ritual and attending a service which has become part of their lives through years of habit.

In another chapter the unique differences in racial tastes for art and literature are found to go back to a native mental endowment. The people, whose attention could grasp many things at once, preferred the more complicated, less obvious styles. This "span of attention" has been a matter of considerable study for some years. An apparatus which exposes a card for a fraction of a second enables the experimenter to learn how many objects can be attended when placed on the card in such a way that the eye inevitably sees them all at the instant of exposure. Considerable differences in the ability to "span" the objects are found in different observers. Why one person's brain should be able to grasp more in a given moment than another's is hard to explain. Perhaps it is due to the physiological ability to arouse brain tracts into activity. If we think of the attention as that part of the brain which is more alert than another part; and if we imagine that this alertness shifts over the brain-tracts, now affecting one centre and now another, awakening groups of associations in the visual centres, in the auditory centres, in the motor areas, or in the speech centres, we may represent to our fancy a class of brains in which the shifting process is slow and the groups of associated tracts are few, or we may imagine the reverse. In those brains which have many tracts active at once we may imagine we have the broad-spanned individual. I am persuaded that such an one not only has a greater area of alertness, but that his faculty for quickly shifting his centre of activity is better than the narrow-spanned.* The broad-spanned attention is apparently the expression of a brain natively endowed in a characteristic way; though the ability to improve in breadth of span is present in all and the narrow type may accomplish much in some one line of endeavour by constant practice.

I recently studied a number of university men with a view to describing the characteristic traits of attention. I found marked differences even among men who had had very much the same sort of educational training for many years. These traits go deeper than education. They are certainly in the very fibres of nature. With the association tests the most marked individualities would appear. Some men would be able to associate four words with a word suggested to them inside of three or four seconds; other men could with difficulty supply the four associated words in twice that time. What a snapshot of the mental processes this gives! When the quick associaters are listening to an address the thoughts move so quickly that they dance all around the lecturer's words; or they will read another volume between a writer's lines. Their world is filled with animation. Thoughts crowd into their minds in throngs. A veritable panorama of ideas ranges before them. Not so with their slow-thinking colleagues. It requires all the time they have to catch and assimilate a speaker's thought. If they attempt to circle around his thought and call up a number of associations to embellish, or illustrate his meaning, the train of thought is lost for

* H. C. McComas: "Some Types of Attention," *Psychol. Monog., 13,* No. 3.

them. They are left behind. But one course is open to them. They must plod.

Surely it must be evident to the most superficial thinker that these two classes of men will gravitate in different directions if left to their own devices. The things that attract and hold the one class will probably not appeal to the other. The mental life in the one is unlike that of the other. With the one those subjects which awaken his mind, and arouse his imagination so that the attention skips through teeming crowds of thoughts will give him a natural satisfaction. The other moves within a narrower horizon. His world is less generously populated. To see at all he must carefully focus upon each thing. A simpler world is his.

It is, of course, impossible to treat all phases of the thinking processes, and it is impracticable to go into many details. Only those large features which obviously affect the individual's intellectual life as it relates to his religious nature interest us. Of these, probably, the "Ideational Types" are most important.

The chapter on "Ideational Types" in psychology is still in the writing. Much remains to be learned. Enough, however, is known about the way in which different people's imagery and memory processes operate to enable us to discriminate between typical groups. In general it may be said that the senses supply the materials which the brain uses in its work. As the infant brain matures the connecting fibres become more and more medullated or sheathed. That is, a sort of insulating of the nerve connections develops with the use of these tracts. Obviously this will not be the same in all brains. Some difference in the proportions of development must arise in the growth of so extremely complex an organ as the brain. Such differences of development added to what innate differences occur in the brain itself would indicate that the later functions of brains could not be identical. With the experiences of different infants, differing, and with the brain predispositions differing, it is but natural to assume that the several senses which furnish the brain with its materials should do so in considerably unequal proportions. One infant may start with a greater facility for catching sounds and retaining them than another. A second may find that it is comparatively easy to remember a movement made and to repeat such a movement in connection with other movements; while, probably, all find that the vast amount of material coming to the brain from the eyes supplies the bulk of the " Thought-Stuff." Some native predisposition, or some exigency of experience, or both, evidently start the brain in its habits. Habits once formed are nature itself. To this moulding of the brain the functions of more mature years bear evidence. For there are very clear differences between the imagery of different people. So clear are these inequalities of mental endowment that the term, *Visualizer,* has been applied to those who represent an experience to the mind clearly and vividly in terms of sight. The *Audile* has an unique ability to recall or imagine tones, noises, a voice, a piece of music, etc. The *Moteur* more easily represents to his mind the feelings in his muscles and joints, lips and throat.

Fechner, one of the great pathfinders in psychology, was the first to study the differences in people's ability to imagine. He compared the visual image which arose in his mind when he thought of a certain object with the clearness and the vividness of the object as it was actually seen. He found that his memory image was nothing like so sharp and coloured as was the actual sight of the object. But he found there were people who could see with their mind's eye memory images which were nearly as distinct as the original subjects. Francis Galton followed the study of these peculiarities with great care. He prepared a set of questions designed to bring out each subject's ability to visualize. To his astonishment he learned that a great many scientists had no knowledge of mental imagery. Their thinking seemed to be in verbal terms. " On the other hand, men and yet a larger number of women, and many boys and girls, declared that they habitually saw mental imagery and that it was perfectly distinct to them and full of colour. The power of visualizing is higher in the female sex than in the male, and is somewhat, but not much, higher in public-school boys than in men. After maturity is reached, the further advance of age does not seem to dim the faculty, but rather the reverse, judging from numerous statements to that effect; but advancing years are sometimes accompanied by hard abstract thinking, and in these cases—not uncommon among those whom I have questioned—the faculty undoubtedly becomes impaired. There is reason to believe that it is very high in some young children, who seem to spend years of difficulty in distinguishing between the subjective and objective world. Language and book-learning certainly tend to dull it. The visualizing faculty is a gift and, like all natural gifts, has a tendency to be inherited. Since families differ so much in respect to this gift, we may suppose that races would also differ, and there can be no doubt that such is the case. I hardly like to refer to civilized nations, because their natural faculties are too much modified by education to allow of their being much appraised in an offhand fashion. I may, however, speak of the French, who appear to possess the visualizing faculty in a high degree. The peculiar ability they show in prearranging ceremonials and fêtes of all kinds, and their undoubted genius for tactics and strategy, show that they are able to foresee effects with unusual clearness. Their ingenuity in all technical contrivances is an additional testimony in the same direction, and so is their singular clearness of expression. Their phrase ' figurez-vous,' or ' picture to yourself,' seems to express their dominant mode of expression."*

Professor James found, after questioning his students for many years, that some could bring a scene before their minds with great distinctness, and that others " have no visual images worthy the name." One poor visualizer said: " My ability to form mental images seems, from what I have studied of other people's images, to be defective, and somewhat peculiar. The process by which I remember any particular event is not by a series of distinct images, but a sort of panorama, the faintest impressions of which are perceptible through a thick fog. I cannot shut my eyes and get a distinct image of anyone, although I used to be able to a few years ago, and the faculty seems to have gradually slipped away."

Professor James declares that " a person whose visual imagination is strong finds it hard to understand how those who are without the faculty can think at all. In some individuals the habitual ' thought-stuff,' if one may

*Quoted by W. James: "The Principles of Psychology," Vol. II, p. 55.

so call it, is visual; in others it is auditory, articulatory, or motor; in most, perhaps, it is evenly mixed. The same local cerebral injury must needs work different practical results in persons who differ in this way. In one it will throw a much-used brain tract out of gear; in another it may affect an unimportant region."

Professor Titchener does not think that the "thought-stuff" is evenly mixed in anyone. I have found but one person in thirty who professed the ability to represent an action to his mind with the distinctness and cogency of sight, and he claimed that his auditory imagery was inferior to either of the other two faculties. I think that most people are visualizers of a higher or lower order in their youth, and that their auditory imagery is next in order of clearness and distinctness, while the motor imagery is least efficient of all. The "Types" result from the fact that the proportions of ability vary from individual to individual, and not from any predominance of auditory or motor imagery over visual, except in abnormal cases, or among the blind.

The auditory Type uses the imagery derived from the sense of hearing very much more than do the other types. The "audile" will seek to retain a page of writing in memory by repeating it aloud and recalling the sound of his voice, rather than by retaining an impression of the appearance of the page. Such people often remember a friend's voice better than his face. Musicians are probably of this type. It is impossible for strong visualizers to conceive how a great musician can hold an image of an entire composition in mind at a given moment.

The "motile" or "moteur" makes use, in memory,

reasoning and all their intellectual operations, of images derived from movement. In order to understand this important point, it is enough to remember " that all our perceptions, and in particular the important ones, those of sight and touch, contain as integral elements the movements of our eyes and limbs; and that, if movement is ever an essential factor in our really seeing an object, it must be an equally essential factor when we see the same object in imagination " (Ribot). There are persons who remember a drawing better when they have followed its outlines with their finger. Lecoq de Boisbaudran used this means in his artistic teaching, in order to accustom his pupils to draw from memory. He made them follow the outlines of figures with a pencil held in the air, forcing them thus to associate muscular with visual memory. Galton quotes a curious corroborative fact. "Colonel Moncrieff often observed in North America young Indians who, visiting occasionally in his quarters, interested themselves greatly in the engravings which were shown them. One of them followed with care with the point of his knife the outline of a drawing in the *Illustrated London News,* saying that this would enable him to carve it out the better on his return home. In this case the motor images were to reënforce the visual ones." *

These differences do not depend upon the sense-organs for their peculiarities. As Titchener says in his " Text-Book of Psychology " (p. 403), " The image is a later development than the sensation, and we may expect, accordingly, that it will show a greater individual variation. The psychology of sensation is concerned primarily

* Binet: " Psychologie du Raisonnement," quoted by James, " Psychology," Vol. II, pp. 60, 61.

with uniformities; all those who possess normal sense-organs have the same general endowment of sensations; and we refer striking peculiarities like colour-blindness, tone-deafness, insensitivity to pitch differences,—we refer these peculiarities, when they appear, to some abnormality of the organ. The psychology of the image, on the other hand, is essentially an individual psychology. The normal brain is a much more variable thing than the normal sense-organ, and the ideas of different minds are constituted in very different ways."

These characteristic modes of recalling the past and of building up images of the external universe undoubtedly account for many dissimilar results in our philosophies and theologies! To quote Titchener again (p. 405), " The attitude of attention is different, according as one is visual or auditory-kinæsthetic; and the mode of recitation differs, being slow and systematic in the former case, quick and impulsive in the latter, while the mistakes made are in both instances characteristic. A preponderant type may be traced in an author's style; and it has been suggested that the cardinal doctrines of the traditional British psychology are to be explained by the fact, evident from their books, that the writers were predominantly visual-minded." Given the same materials out of which to build great conceptions, so differently will widely unlike types of mind handle these materials that the structures built will be as far apart as the Colosseum and an epic poem. If philosophy could start with axioms which were grounded upon fundamental laws of thought, and could build upon such a foundation while adhering to rigid logical principles, all philosophy would result in the same conclusions. Types of imagination and of attention would have no more influence upon such systems than they do upon mathematics.* Our starting points in philosophy are chosen in harmony with our mental tastes. Our tastes are satisfied only as our thinking proceeds along congenial lines.

Two of the most noted philosophers of to-day live side by side. They are old friends. Each has read the other's books and is conversant with his philosophy. Both have remarkably clear minds and great ability of expression. Each succeeds in persuading many highly-educated, brilliant minds to accept his system of philosophy. Neither succeeds in convincing the other that the other's system is wrong. Why? If philosophy were grounded solely upon facts, either of these master-minds would readily correct his system to fit the facts. If philosophy were a rigid structure of logic both of these minds would follow the same route and arrive at the same destination. Philosophy does deal with facts and does use logic, but not exclusively. It is an interpretation of the universe. Of what universe? Obviously each mind knows best the universe of his own experience and observation. To the broad-spanned, the universe is full of rich colours, wondrous forms, unnumbered suggestions of things not known or knowable, to the narrow-spanned, known by symbol rather than in warm, living colour, by words rather than by objects; but incisive, sharp and cleanly cut.

These psychological types of mind afford an explanation for the tendency of the German to explain the universe in terms of mystery or in great systems of Idealism; while his French neighbour loves positivism and the clear, clean-cut thinking of Realism. They also help

* Stern, L. W.: "Ueber Psychologie der Indiv. Differenzen," pp. 52, 53.

us to understand why the study of life in the splendid systems of philosophy, from Thales down, is so full of contradictions. A study of these philosophers' theories of the attention shows that they were not all of the same type, and where it is possible to learn of their ideational type there are strong indications of diversity there.*

Along with these mental traits go certain traits of quickness or slowness in mental activity. "There are also marked individual differences of association. Observers in the psychological laboratory fall, as do children in the schoolroom, into two great groups; the quick learners and the slow learners. Popular psychology has been all on the side of the slow pupil; if he is slow, he is also sure; his knowledge is solidly established; while his more active-minded companion is pronounced shallow; his knowledge goes as easily as it comes. Retention, we have no need to insist, is a very complicated matter, and there may very well be conditions under which popular psychology is right. Experiments seem to show, however, that at least under certain circumstances it is definitely wrong. The quick learner appears to retain as well as the slow; he has the advantage at the start, and he loses nothing by the lapse of time." †

Without adding to the list of mental traits enough have been discussed to give a very good explanation of several types of religious thinking. But, before considering the results of these native endowments upon the beliefs of their possessors, a few words should be devoted to the place of *thinking* in a man's religion.

It is very often said that theology is not religion, that creed and dogma obstruct rather than assist re-

* L. L. Uhl: "On Attention."
† Titchener, *op. cit.*, p. 405.

ligious progress. No one can deny that a theology which commended itself to people who did not know the simple truths of geography, astronomy, history, chemistry, biology and psychology with which a high-school pupil of to-day is familiar, is a theology that gives more perplexity than clarity in religious thinking. Not only is the teaching at variance with modern knowledge, but the spirit of the sixteenth century could tolerate a despotic, Calvinistic deity which is intolerable to American, modern ideals. It is true, therefore, that our inherited theologies and creeds do not help educated people, and often are the causes of disaster. Be that as it is! That does not prove that systematic, consistent statements are not great aids to thought in any sphere, religious or other. A system of theology which commands *intelligent* assent is the great demand of this age. For one thing is indisputably true, no one can *think* one thing and *believe* another. Moreover, no one can have a religion which does not rest on a *creed,* not definite, perhaps, but definite enough for him to know what, in general, he thinks about God, the Soul, Duty and the Future. Every religious experience must have some thought-basis. It is absurd to say " away with theology, let us have religion." It would be as sensible to say " away with the mere objects of affection, let us have affection alone, supreme." No emotion, no spiritual experience can take hold upon a man unless his thoughts first arouse the latent powers of his nature. Once awakened, they accompany his thoughts, helping to colour and to fashion them. The more emotional he is the more the aroused feelings will lead his thinking; the more intellectual he is, the more his emotions will be controlled by his thinking. In his thinking he will take the direction his nature imposes.

As the traveller, who does not know that nature usually gives a man one leg slightly shorter than the other, walks in the forests, or on the prairies, always tends to turn toward the side of the shorter limb; so the thinker unconsciously veers into the direction which his individual traits decree. Some men are liberal, some are literal in their thought-lives. Beneath the actual results of their thinking the undertow of nature may be detected as it urges them in one general direction.

From what has been said, it is not hard to group certain mental traits together and to predict what will be the trend of the thinker possessing them. The ability to learn quickly means the ability to recall easily what has been learned before. Associations arise quickly; they surround the new impression, they give it its interpretation, they give it a place in company with many other impressions received before. Some men associate so quickly that they cannot begin to express themselves as quickly as their thoughts come flooding in. Others speak slowly and, on introspecting, declare that they have expressed every thought that occurred to them. When the associations come in terms of visual imagery we often speak of the person as *imaginative,* though the word is as applicable to any other form of imagery. Some authors describe the conception of their work as coming before their mental vision in throngs of scenes. Spurgeon once said that his imagination gave the thunderous hoof-beats of a host of horses so distinctly that he seemed actually to hear them. To a mind which calls up many impressions of a character similar to the one being received the new one is broadened and heightened. To the slower thinker this may also occur if he has the time for it; but if he is listening to a sermon he will not have the time, and his impression of what the speaker has said will be very much slimmer and more colourless than that of his quicker neighbour. The mental habits of the two become dissimilar. The mind that ranges easily and quickly over many thoughts will acquire a habit of looking at propositions from many points of view. So many possibilities occur that a breadth of view, a tolerance of different ideas, becomes natural. If we add to this mental alertness the faculty of grasping ideas in the large, as the broad-spanned type was seen to do, we have an additional reason for a *liberal* mind. For with such a faculty a statement tends to come not piecemeal but wholly before the mind. The unity of the thought is apprehended. One notices such differences in giving dictation to a stenographer. Some grasp a long sentence, holding the thought in all of its relations; while others can take only a clause at a time. More painfully does one notice it when, after a public address or sermon, some hearers show their comprehension of the thoughts expressed and some show they have only fragments, which they quote literally, showing an entirely different understanding of what was said. Surely, these two classes of minds see two different religious worlds.

It must not be supposed that the liberal mind is the issue of intellectual factors alone. Feeling always enters. Sometimes a broad, quick intellect is found holding the convictions of the Literalist and using his gifts to defend them. If we add to our breadth of attention and alertness of thought an emotional nature, which is not intense enough to over-ride the intellect, but which is vigorous enough to sympathize with the feelings of others,—a nature which has known love, fear, anger, hope, sorrow and happiness; then the scope of the mental life is supplemented by that of feeling and the outcome is the Liberal.

To a mind of such endowments the narrative of Christ's Last Supper will teem with life. It will be impossible to satisfy such a nature with a partial understanding of the narration. No "mass" or "close communion" would ever occur to his mind in reading the account. The narrowed outlook, which sees in the supper one thing and that only, is impossible to a liberal nature reading the narrative without prejudice. For him the *whole* scene rises as a whole; the character of the feast, its history, the hostile city, the fidelity and infidelity of the men present, the wonderful soul that illumines the whole event, the spirit of the hour, the teaching of the Leader, His rebuke to their ambitions, His washing of the disciples' feet, His love for them all, His giving them the bread and wine, His reaching into the same bowl with Judas, both eating the same morsels, the avowal of loyalty, the impending tragedy. From such a climax, in the career of Christ, only the Literalist could wrench the isolated teaching of "feet washing," or "transubstantiation." So, indeed, throughout the Bible the mind and heart which see and feel largely will take more than single passages, proof texts, or specific incidents for the bases of their religious beliefs.

In contrast with this we may group the traits opposite in character to those which went into the making of the Liberal. If one learns slowly he cannot in the same length of time learn as much as the quick learner. At thirty years of age he will not be as well informed as the quick thinker of the same age—other things being equal. He may give the impression of having learned thor-

INTELLECTUAL TYPES

oughly what he has, because he brings his mental possessions into small compass and can give good epitomes of what he knows. The clearness of his knowledge, due to his singleness of viewpoints, passes for solidity and accuracy. This is the slow-thinking, narrow-spanned mind with no crowding, teeming imagery. Add to such a mental constitution an emotional nature that takes its bias very largely from its intellectual convictions, and that does not readily change its emotional attitude. (Not infrequently, however, the emotional type that feels strongly, with lasting likes and dislikes, is coupled with the narrower intellectual type.) Here, then, are very probable ingredients of the character known as the Literalist.

To the Literalist things *are* what they seem. To him the Scriptures say what they say and naught beside. A translation from Horace must give an English equivalent for each Latin word. What the ancient poet said must be repeated verbally in English. Then the Literalist has line for line the ancient ode; but the humour and the subtle innuendoes have all escaped. The Literalist must have just what Jesus said. To see *humour* in the story of the man straining gnats out of his wine and drinking down a camel is to see what is not in Christ's words—for the Literalist. To find a Saviour who cannot be known part by part is impossible to the mind that is forced to think in fractions. It takes what it can, few associations rise to relate its new impression with its old. No vistas of suggestion open deep perspectives and numerous relations. Things stand alone. Relations are few. The slow and narrow-spanned mind apprehends what it can and tries to relate what it holds in terms that are within its compass. It makes for clearness. It finds logic a good support. It seeks to arrange its findings in a logical, clear order, that they may be grasped easily. Truths that are too great to be reduced to formal statements are not truths for the Literalist, they are vagaries. The many-sided truths of the Scriptures are stripped of their sides. Three-dimensional truths are made simple linear truths, in order to connect them together and to give an intelligible little whole.

The Literalist does not miss the higher and wider truths of life because he wishes to do so. He cannot help it. He serves his fellows by keeping them from undue expansion and its resulting shallowness. He injures his cause by clinging to the little he can find, and defending it against larger issues and against growth and change. He does not grow. He does not feel the need for growing. He has his whole Truth. It satisfies him. He does not move. Then he should never attempt to lead. But he does attempt it,—unfortunately.

From what has been said concerning imagery it is possible to interpret a disposition (among people of widely separated denominations) to use a ritual in their church services. We have seen that the thinking of many people is quite strongly imaginal. This is especially so if they have not done a great deal of abstract thinking. To such imaginative minds the truths which awaken emotional response and which sustain the spiritual life may well be presented by impressions upon the senses. These impressions afford the pigments for the imagination to paint its portrayals of the truths imparted in the services. It is surprising to find how much of our thinking is full of imagery.* Anything that helps to

*J. R. Angell: "Imageless Thought," *Psychological Review, 18,* pp. 295-323.

make spiritual truths part of one's life is certainly of value. This seems to be a growing conviction in many churches. Puritan churches, which for generations lived on the sermons and the prayers, are giving more and more of their services to ritual. One cannot read the introspection of anyone strongly of the motor type without seeing the important part that movements play in his thinking.* To kneel helps many to bring their thoughts into a devotional line, to repeat responses aids many in fixing their minds upon a lofty theme; to rise, to bow, to kneel in unison brings the conception of fellowship to some who would otherwise not acquire it.

Such, then, are a few of the elements which go into the making of the intellectual side of the religious nature. More there may be; but for the argument of this book these are sufficient.

The next step is to look again at the different Natural Sects and to discover how applicable are these psychological principles to the types found there.

* Rodolfo Mondolfo: "Studi sui tipi rappresentativi," *Riv. di filos.*, 1909, *15*, pp. 39-92.

XII

THE INDIVIDUAL AND HIS SECT

WE have seen the same truths, now, from several angles of view. We have seen the answers of a number of religious people to the questions concerning the bases of their faith; and in those answers it was clear that some found their religious experiences centring around intellectual statements, and convictions; while others found their religious life welling up from what seemed to be life itself, from the fountain-head of life, the emotions, affections; while others took their religion from "authority," or from the habits of their early life, and merely accepted what they found, following their habitual impulse and imitating others. Among philosophers the same three kinds of centres gathered their peculiar kinds of definitions of religion. One set found religion in the intellectual life; another set found it in the feelings; and a third found it in conduct or activity. This last set would correspond to the intellectual-action type. Now, in the history of the sects we saw how those sects which were *Natural* sects and were the outcome of forces at work within their own natures, showed the same disposition to express their religion in three kinds. One set of sects emphasized beliefs, doctrines; a second laid the stress on the experience of the convert, the spiritual, the emotional life of the follower of Christ; while a third called out

THE INDIVIDUAL AND HIS SECT

the impulses and aroused the instinctive responses in their followers. A study of human nature showed how the different periods in an individual's life shifted the balance of the forces controlling his nature. In the early years instinct and imitation are the chief factors. In youth the emotional nature asserts itself, while in maturity the intellectual dominates. A further study of these three great characteristics of human nature showed a number of minor traits coupled with the larger. The task in the present chapter is a very difficult one. It is nothing less than the characterization of each of the important denominations according to its more conspicuous natural traits.

Such a hazardous undertaking must be *suggestive* only. It cannot be absolutely accurate. Many misinterpretations must creep in despite every effort. Nevertheless, so broad and so evident are many of the characteristics of a number of these sects that it is not difficult to characterize them. Of course, what is said of a sect as a whole does not apply to every individual in it. Indeed, a very large number of the members of any denomination may be of quite a different type from that assigned to the sect as a whole. Then, too, the sects are changing in many of their peculiarities. What was very true of them a few decades ago is not so true now. However, it is quite practicable to assign a general character to many distinctive sects and to indicate roughly what sort of an emotional, intellectual and practical life they have.

With these cautions in mind a number of sects are described below. These descriptions are based on the history of the sect, the character of its service, its creeds, activities, interests and personnel.

The Adventists were originallly an impulsive-emotional people. They acted out the expectation which had been awakened in them. They were imitative. The contagion of their fear and hope spread widely, among their type. They were not dominantly intellectual,—or the ideas of the farmer, William Miller, would never have taken hold upon them. They passed from the heat of this early excitement, when Miller's predictions proved false. Then the denomination settled into the emotional-doctrinal type, letting the enthusiasm which gave the sect birth gather around the conceptions of Christ's coming and the seventh day as a Sabbath.

The Adventists are a very good example of a common process in church history. First comes the overwhelming emotionalism, then reconstruction and a gathering of certain doctrines and beliefs peculiar to the movement. After this the settling and hardening of these beliefs into the mainstay of the church. This latter stage is the dogmatic.

A typical Adventist is not of the alert, quick, mental type, with a wide range of intellectual interests. He is directed in his thought life and held to his beliefs very largely by his feelings. His *experience* of religion expresses itself in actions of a certain kind, i.e., observances of his church. It is not the tumultuous emotion of the revivalist, or the subdued emotion of the intellectualist; but rather the emotion incident to, as well as productive of, his beliefs. He is usually of the dogmatic type.

The Baptists comprise many bodies, and some shifting in accentuation of traits occurs as one reviews the different bodies. So great is the membership that all

THE INDIVIDUAL AND HIS SECT 189

sections of the United States are represented. This gives a difference in the spirit of different branches of the church. The more rigid doctrinaires are found in the *Primitive Baptist* churches, which are most numerous in Virginia, North Carolina, Georgia and Tennessee. In the North the Calvinism is not so strong.*

Throughout the Baptist bodies there are these general tendencies: an insistence upon the letter of the Scriptures in such matters as Immersion, Infant Baptism and Close Communion; that is, an insistence upon certain isolated teachings of the Bible adhered to in a literal way. This is the mark of the Literalist. The type of mind which can survey the canons of the Old and New Testaments and discriminate values, grasp the vital spirit of the whole, and subordinate the particular to the general, is not a type which animates the entire Baptist Church to-day. Baptist religion is the issue in many parts of the denomination. This makes for a centrifugal sort of a life. The young people were encouraged to start their own organizations when the Young People's Christian Endeavour Societies sought to gather in all young people of all denominations.

The genuine Baptist is not the wide-visioned type; his mind gravitates to particulars. He varies in his emotional nature from the conversion type (which passes through a definite religious experience), to the emotional-dogmatic type (which lives in the attachment to certain creeds).

THE CHRISTIANS (*Christian Connection*) are a very good, representative American sect; they reflect the aver-

* See A. H. Newman: "A History of the Baptist Churches in the United States."

age qualities of the American people very well. It is a sect which has grown up with the Middle West. Three other sects, the Presbyterian, Baptist and Methodist, entered into its origin. Each of these separated from its parent body in the effort to get a greater freedom. Later they discovered that they had much in common and formed a union. Unity among Christians has been one of their chief tenets. They hold to no creed or confession to give unity to their sect, but rely upon the Christian's life and religious nature to supply the binding ties. In their earlier career they were more emotional than to-day,—witness, the influence of Millerism upon their order.

Intellectually, the Christians, while sympathetic and open to other conceptions than their own, are not of a vigorous, constructive type. The intellectual life is not of primary importance. But the life of "experience" is of great importance. This does not make for the conversion type so much as for a more stable, uniform, emotional life. The emotion is not of the austere character, but rather of the wholesome, optimistic sort, which is congenial to a new and growing section of the country.

COLOURED DENOMINATIONS are very much the same in religious type whatever name they may assume. As they have been discussed before, all that need be said here is that they are of the conversion-emotional type, subject to impulse and to imitation. They are imitating the churches of the white people, in the large cities, and this coupled with an improvement in education, makes for a more sober and uniform life than is seen where their native impulses are given greater freedom.

THE CHRISTIAN SCIENCE MOVEMENT has been described from the viewpoint of this book. It remains to be added that Christian Science has recruited its membership, not from rural communities nor from the illiterate of the cities, but from people in many sects in many cities; often from the wealthy classes. The intellectual factor may well be this, many people have been brought up to believe creeds which are very hard to hold in later years, Christian Science offers an escape from the puzzling creeds! Furthermore, the mind that could accept some of the ultra-orthodox creeds is prepared to accept the strange tenets of Mrs. Eddy. Nevertheless, the intellectual element is not the actuating one in drawing recruits. Rather the emotional and the auto-suggestible nature is the chief promoter,—and such a nature is often found in all classes of society, but it is not a usual accompaniment of a strong intellectual power.

The Christian Scientist is of the impulsive, emotional type and the intellectual, literalist type.

THE CONGREGATIONALISTS have gone in an opposite direction to that taken by many sects. For instead of starting with emotional enthusiasm and cooling down to doctrinal statements of what they should hold as infallible rules of faith and practice, their past history has been replete with doctrine and theology, while their present life is absorbed in ethical, educational and devotional interests.

The average Congregationalist is alert intellectually, with broad interests and a sympathetic outlook upon other faiths than his own. Emotionally, he believes himself to be above emotionalism. His interest in education emphasizes this. But there is an emotional life in the sect which expresses itself in a number of practical ways, and, also, in the æsthetic side of the church services. It is not the conversion type or the dogmatic type, but a type which arises naturally in connection with broad intellectual interests and a vigorous altruism. The Congregationalist is liberal-minded, with an optimistic emotional trait. His church spreads easily in the North and West, but does not take root in the South.

THE DISCIPLES OF CHRIST is another sect which has thriven with the Middle West, and which is representative of the spirit of fraternity in this country. Though it sprang from Baptist sources and holds to some Baptist peculiarities, it is avowedly without a creed. The Bible alone is its faith. It holds as one of its cherished convictions the unity of the churches.

The membership is of average American people. It is not of a strongly intellectual cast, but it is open-minded and tolerant in rather a larger measure than is to be expected in a body which adheres rather strictly to the letter of a part of the Scripture. It is hardly fair to say it is of the Literal type; nor yet, of the obviously Liberal. Emotionally, it is of the experiential, not the impulsive, or the dogmatic, type; with the wholesome fervour which makes for expansion and improvement.

A division from the Disciples appears in the *Churches of Christ*. This sect is composed of members who were not comfortable among the Disciples. They resented the growth of agencies to assist in church work or service, such as missionary societies, or instrumental music. Eventually they separated from the other body. Here is a clear case of difference in religious types. With the same heritage and in the same age, under the same general influences one type tends in one direction, the other in another.

Intellectually, this division is more of the Literalist type than its parent body. It seeks a "Thus saith the Lord" for its support. It claims to speak only of what the Scriptures speak. It is moved by the desire for particulars, for details; rather than for the large and inclusive spirit which leaves details to the individual judgment. In the emotional sphere there is less of the optimistic wholesomeness and more of the austere introspection.

THE DUNKERS are the descendants of the splendid movement which sought to put real, religious life into that barren period of church history which succeeded the Reformation. The two largest bodies of Dunkers in America are the Conservative and the Progressive. Among the Conservatives there is a strict adherence to the letter of the Scripture. As Jesus washed His disciples' feet so do the Dunkers. Jesus' dress was simple, theirs is very plain. Jesus had no home, they eschew all finery in a house, such as carpets and pictures. In the times of Christ the sick were anointed with oil; this, also, the Dunkers do. When Christ was crucified His head fell forward. When the Dunkers baptize it is with the head forward. The educational interests are centred very thoroughly upon the Bible.

Here, then, is a Literalism of a rather thoroughgoing kind. It has selected a group of incidents around which it builds its life. The isolation of the Dunkers, also, makes for a narrow horizon intellectually. Emotionally they are not of the explosive type but rather of the dogmatic-emotional type. This expresses itself not so much in creeds as in an everyday activity.

The Progressive branch does not insist on different ideas but upon a release from the restriction of the organization, so that each member shall have more freedom. The movement is more in keeping with the age. Its natural outcome is to get rid of the bizarre and to conform more to the times. The Progressives are nearer to the "intellectual-emotional" side of the series of types and further from the "action-emotional" than the Conservatives.

THE EVANGELICAL ASSOCIATION grew up from the labours of Jacob Albright, who was converted and had a profound religious experience when he was thirty years of age. The chief interest of the sect is in the spiritual life, in a development which is known as "Sanctification." In this state of feeling one cares nothing for the temptations to yield to other pleasures. The "peace, joy and rest" of this state are of such worth that nothing can purchase them. The doctrines are simple and orthodox. The educational interests are limited.

This is primarily an experiential type. It is nearer the impulsive, the instinctive end of the scale of emotional types than to the intellectual end. The ecstatic experiences are sometimes of the nature of motor-automatisms. It is of the cheerful, hopeful character of emotion rather than the austere and repressive. It enjoys a wonderful experience which is a source of strength and delight, and it wishes to spread this treasure abroad. Intellectually there is little of moment; the intellectual life being led by the emotional.

THE INDIVIDUAL AND HIS SECT

The Friends of to-day are divided and dissimilar in several particulars. The conservative wing is certainly of a more emotional, experiential type than the progressive wing. The "Inner Light" means more to a man prompted by feelings than to one who is guided more by his thinking. The progressive element express their religion more by ethical and educational work than in their devotional experience.

The Latter-day Saints have lost the fervour and the excess of the originators. Their religious life centres around practical and executive matters rather than spiritual experience. Education has received considerable attention and encouragement. The type of member is not broad, intellectually, but rather the literalist type, and the dogmatic-emotional.

The Lutherans, with their twenty-four bodies, are alike in holding to doctrine as preëminent. Justification before God by means of faith is the central conviction. "Faith" is not merely a matter of intellectual assent but also an emotional matter in that the believer accepts Christ in a personal way. Their church history is full of theological battles. The understanding of doctrines has been of first importance. Education is encouraged, and the education of the youth in the doctrines of the church is a prominent part of the church work; for the child is brought up to pass from the Sunday-school to the church as a natural process,—no radical religious experience being expected.

The type is in the nature of the literal which makes for a dogmatic adherence to established doctrines and the emotional life is around these conceptions.

THE METHODISTS show a range of religious types from the impulsive, explosive member in a Southern country church to the sedate, orderly attendant in a Northern city. Wherever a Methodist worships the chief feature is the spiritual life, however, and not a doctrinal conviction, or a special ritual, or an order of observances.

Intellectually the type is alert and imaginative. But abstract thinking, or concentrated, persistent thinking upon the subjects of their faith is not characteristic. First in their interest is the conversion of the sinner and the *experience* of religion. This experience is sometimes violent, sometimes gentle, but it is definite enough to be recognized. The emotional nature is rather of the expansive, cheerful sort than the austere, and seeks to hold the Christian to the life of devotion by its attractiveness rather than by instilling a hatred of "worldliness." It is, in general, a conversion-emotional type.

THE PRESBYTERIAN CHURCH history is full of the clash of doctrines. It is a church whose origin expressed a logical system of faith. Calvin's orderly convictions have always been in the foreground of the church. It has appealed to the intellectual side of its followers in a peculiar way. It has not followed the purely intellectual course of leaving matters open to reasoning, but has asserted its premises and demanded an acceptance. There is a type of mind which can formulate doctrines and, by an act of the will rather than the judgment, adopt them as true. This, the Scotch-Irish can do. Having accepted them, it is a matter of determination rather than reason how long they shall be held. One early Presbyterian prayed, "Grant that I may always be right, for Thou knowest I am hard to turn." Those early Presbyterians insisted upon an educated ministry, and insisted to such an extent that the church suffered. This dogmatic nature varies in its types. In a controversy of the last century, which resulted in a division in the sect, such a difference appeared. " When the separation was complete it was found that the new school embraced about four-ninths of the ministry and membership of the church, mostly lying in the Northern States. It coincided in the main with the lines of discrimination between Scotch-Irish and New England elements, as it grew largely out of the incompatibility of their tempers."*

The intellectual type is rather of the narrow type, insisting upon a distinct, logical clearness of conceptions rather than large, broad, elastic conceptions. It is literal rather than poetic (op. cit., p. 220). The emotional side is a product of the intellectual rather than productive of it. Consequently the sect easily becomes dogmatic. Of course the levelling influences of the age smooth away many of the conspicuous features which showed in the earlier history of the sect.

THE PROTESTANT EPISCOPAL CHURCH contains many different kinds of religious natures. It calls for no striking religious experience and makes no great demands upon intellectual assent to difficult doctrines. A child of Episcopal parents naturally grows up into the church whether he be strongly emotional or intellectual. The history of the church in this country is rather free from doctrinal battles and emotional crises. There are general trends toward High Church or Low Church,

* R. E. Thompson: "The Presbyterians," p. 120.

which may indicate the native preferences of the membership as it is appealed to æsthetically, or intellectually.

The typical Episcopalian should be the type which is aided in his thinking and feeling by participation in action, the motor type of ideation. He should be the imaginative type responsive to the appeals to his æsthetic nature. Abstract, logical thought need not be an asset. Deep emotional experience is not called for. Many classes can and are attracted to the services of this sect. While many others find it intolerable; as it does not appeal strongly enough to the emotions, or rigorously enough to the mind, to suit them.

THE UNITARIAN CHURCH, concerning which so much has already been said, needs a very brief notice only to be given here.

Many people who find they cannot hold the beliefs of their youth find a church home among the Unitarians. This tends to keep the intellectual feature in the foreground and to emphasize a difference between Unitarians and other churches. The interest of the church is cultural, educational and ethical. It looks for salvation through the growth in the individual's character. It is primarily intellectual and the emotions are æsthetic.

THE UNITED BRETHREN were the outgrowth of the energetic work of Otterbein in the last of the eighteenth century. His was a deeply spiritual nature and he impressed the need of a devout life upon his followers. The church divided about twenty-five years ago and has its progressive and conservative wings, as do so many other sects. In character it is largely Methodist, with which body it has been closely related. Its first labours were among the German people in Pennsylvania and Maryland, and there are many of German extraction in the membership to-day.

It is not of a dominantly intellectual type. The intellectual life is rather subordinated to the religious experience. It is an experiential type and tends rather to the conversion type than the dogmatic.

THE UNIVERSALIST CHURCHES have much in common with the Unitarian. They have rather more doctrinal interest and less broad educational aspirations. Emotionally they are rather more responsive than the Unitarians, and have rallied around their doctrinal contentions concerning the future life in a manner rather characteristic of the dogmatic-emotional type. They are like the several other sects in which we could not discover any vigorous emotional or intellectual life. Perhaps, like these other sects, they do not put much of their life into their religion.

These brief descriptions are nothing more than outline sketches. They include only the broad, clear tracings which give form and character. When they are arranged in the order of progression from the impulsive, imitative Action Types up to the altruistic Intellectual Types their similarities and dissimilarities can easily be compared. In the table below the several headings must not be understood as distinct and separate from each other; for they should, of course, run into each other. No sharp lines can be drawn between the types and sub-types, and the headings indicate merely a *prominence* of the feature described. Thus the imitative-instinctive type shades into the suggestible, especially into an auto-suggestible type. This passes into a stage where the emotional nature, which runs through all the types, is effective in bringing changes into the religious life through conversions. This conversion type melts away into a type more given to controlling its emotions intellectually but with an active emotional disposition. This, in turn, fades into a type in which the intellect seeks to hold what the emotions have found satisfying or when the emotions are enlisted in what the intellect has found acceptable. From such a type we proceed into a type which lets the intellectual shape the religious life, in very large measure, and which exercises more refined and æsthetic than strong and moving emotions, altruism being one mode of expression for its emotions, and the series ends in a strongly intellectual nature which overrides both the æsthetic and altruistic.

The line beside the name of each sect indicates the religious type or types under which it is classed. Thus, the Baptists range from the Conversion and the Emotional Types to the Dogmatic. In several cases a continued dotted line signifies that a small proportion of the sect is to be found in the several Types under which the line runs.

This arrangement shows at a glance the relations of the different sects to each other when they are classified according to their psychological characteristics. Thus, the old story is told once more. That the emotional nature is the mainspring of the religious life and that the religion of all the sects is "touched with emotion." The prominence of other qualities in conjunction with emotion appears in many sects which are socially and historically wide apart. In a number of cases the

THE INDIVIDUAL AND HIS SECT

DENOMINATIONS	ACTION TYPES	EMOTIONAL TYPES	INTELLECTUAL TYPES
	Instinctive and Imitative.	Suggestible, Conversional, Emotional.	Dogmatic, Altruistic and Æsthetic, Intellectual

Adventists ....
Baptists ....
Catholics ....
Christian Connection ...
Coloured Churches......
Christian Science ......
Congregational ....
Disciples of Christ ....
Churches of Christ ...
Dunkards:
   Conservative ....
   Progressive ....
Evangelical Association.
Friends:
   Conservative.........
   Progressive..........
Latter-day Saints ......
Lutheran...............
Methodist ....
Presbyterian ....
Protestant Episcopal ...
Unitarian..............
United Brethren ....
Universalist...........

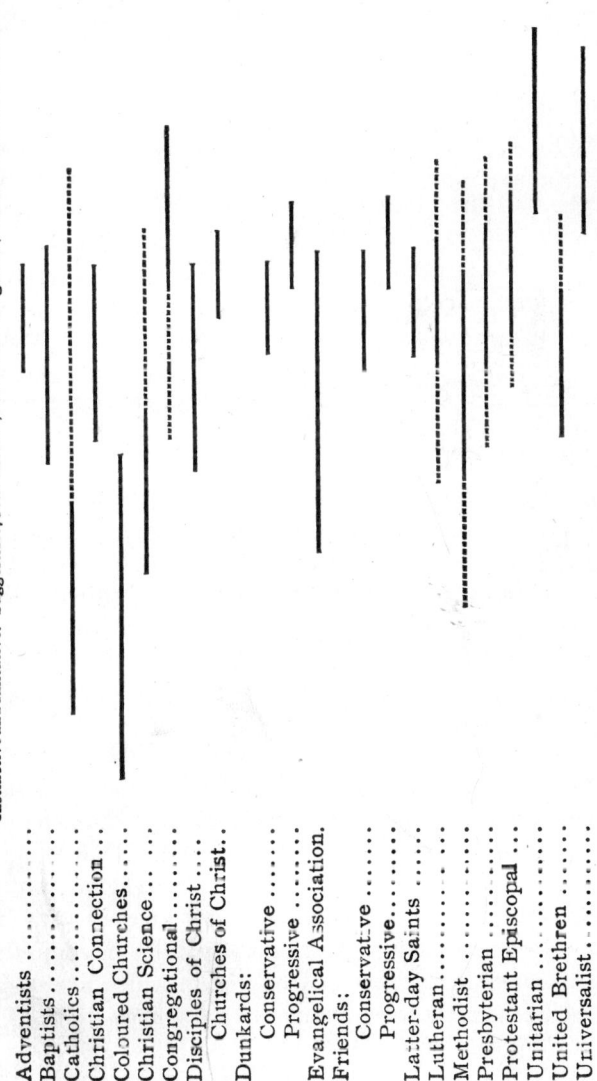

religious types are quite close together. But the tenets they hold are far apart, so far, indeed, that the real similarities of the types are obscured in ordinary observation.

The table cannot show all the relations of the sects in all their traits. The very scheme of the arrangement precludes that. Also, the traits of the Literalist and of the Liberal are not shown. It is not designed to tell any such an exact story as Mendeléeff's table of chemical elements, where the character of the elements changes as you read across the table, and changes with precision and certainty. Our table is *suggestive* of great, though subtle relations. Time and research will unquestionably modify it in many details, but not in the general truths which it obviously teaches.

XIII

LEVELLING FORCES

IN nature the most conspicuous forces are the cataclysmic forces. They rend and heave and twist the rocks and lift the mountain crags. Less spectacular are the forces which level down; they smooth the hills away and fill the valley hollows. The great forces that make for irregularity are met the world over by the forces which make for regularity. The mountain heights are slowly swept away to make the level fields of the valley.

So in society, war disrupts, immigration thrusts in new social strata, dissension gives rise to opposing parties; these and other forces make the differences in the social order. Opposing them are the forces which heal differences, smooth over disparities, that both level up and level down.

In the preceding chapters the differences between religious people were emphasized at considerable length. The way in which the differences of the Old World came over into the American Church, the way in which the Civil War disrupted the Church, the schisms of polity and doctrine and, most important of all, the natural differences in human nature, were all presented and fully discussed. In the midst of these descriptions of disruptions and secessions nothing was said of the great agencies which are at work in healing the scars of conflict and in bringing peace and harmony among those whose differences arise in so many ways.

In this chapter some of these levelling forces will be pointed out as they spread in society in general, and in the Church in particular.

In America unquestionably the public school is the greatest institution for levelling down differences in the social order. Here the English language is an indispensable means of bringing the children of all nations together in thought. It is the vehicle of Anglo-Saxon ideas, ideals and achievements. With the same language children whose parents came from Northern Europe and from Southern Europe enter into the literature of America. It is of the very first importance that the newcomers to our shores think their thoughts in our language as well as receive their thoughts from our literature; for a common language helps to mould thoughts in common. Other studies are taken up by the children of all countries and from all kinds of homes, and together they mature in their education. This maturity is something they share with each other, they feel they have grown in their intellectual lives and that their growth is a possession which they hold in common. Working together makes for mutual understanding and mutual good-feeling. In the recreation hours these children with their diverse heritages mingle and engage in those games which are characteristic of American children; games which call for fair play, for treating each player upon the basis of his natural merits only. There is no place for pretensions here. Quick wits and good muscles, whether possessed by Swede or Italian, make the leaders. The most important factor is the teacher. From her the best that America has to give is imparted to the young. Often these public-school teachers are women and men of very fine character. More than their information is imparted to their pupils; their good nature, frankness, civility and even courage are contagious. Thus, a number of subtle forces play upon the future citizens of the nation and smooth down the differences incident to birth; and impart many qualities which in later life mark them as typical Americans. These youths often come to our colleges and universities, and so thoroughly has the work of the public schools been done that it is impossible to tell what nationality is represented if it were not for some peculiarity in the names, which tell the story of ancestors' homes in Scotland, Sweden, Germany or other lands.

After school life, when these children of foreign parents begin to earn a living, they naturally drop into organizations; trade or labour unions, social and fraternal orders. In every society the "peculiar man" is taboo. So the unusual individual seeks to imitate the ideas and feelings of his fellows. He merges into his set and becomes a part of the great whole.

Less visible are the unorganized agencies, especially what is called "social pressure." Fashion is the great example of this. The styles of ten years ago seem absurd, they actually look ugly; styles of to-day are undoubtedly just as ugly. Why do they not appear so ugly? The reason seems to be that great numbers of people approve them; what is admired by many becomes a standard for the individual and a sort of mutual assistance is rendered, each one lending another aid in admiring the unadmirable. So of important things. Beliefs which fifteen years ago were extravagant are now quite possible. Many a man who held that the tenets of socialism were unthinkable admits to-day "that there is something in them." Or, to go still further back, how hard it is to imagine the convictions of a slaveholder; though we know that excellent and educated people did own slaves. Public opinion, the social mind, brings individuals into line. Not ideas alone, but taste may be imparted by public opinion. Compare the plays, operas, newspapers and recreations of different peoples at different times. The æsthetic feelings may be cultivated in an individual by his social surroundings. Not a few people have acquired a taste for classical music because others of their social set frequented the operas. The moral feelings, too, are educated in the individual by the society in which he lives; there is to-day a growing sentiment concerning the responsibility of each individual to his fellowmen. One can detect the increase of this sentiment in the last two decades. We must conclude, therefore, that our age impresses certain ideas upon the minds of people and also inspires them with certain feelings. In both the intellectual and the emotional life social environment manufactures citizens of a certain great type. How easy it is to detect an American abroad! How quickly we recognize his thoughts and his feelings; they are so characteristic of the nation from which he comes.

This social environment exercises its influence only where there is a certain density of population. In thinly settled parts of the country there is very little of this. Cities are the centres of social influence. Isolation assists individuality and increases, or at least maintains, diverse types. Communication, constant interchange of thoughts and purposes, shape people to mutual resemblances. The cities tend to fashion their inhabitants after one general pattern, giving them certain fashions, manners, customs, morals and ideas. A new conception will spread through the inhabitants of a city and leap to other cities. The American Revolution, the movement against slavery, the single tax, socialism, all originated and gathered headway in the cities. Of old, Christianity spread first through the cities. The country people, the *pagani,* were the pagans.

What bearing has all this upon the religious life? How does it affect the problem of the Sects? It shows that, despite the various ideas advocated by the different denominations, there are forces at work which are slowly clearing away these differences. The public schools are giving the citizens of the country a common attitude toward the questions of life. Men who have been educated from the same books are very apt to acquire the same way of looking at things. Millerism could not spread to-day as it did a half-century ago. The education of the times would not support it. Some conceptions spread easily and widely through our nation because they are congenial to the conceptions which were inculcated during the years of education. Others can make no headway at all among the American people.

Among the leaders of the Church this sameness of education has had a very beneficent influence. I recall a group of clergymen, Baptists, Congregationalists, Presbyterians and Methodists, who were in thorough accord in their thoughts and purposes. Their training in school, college and university had been much the same, and their habits of thought were naturally very much alike. Among laymen the schools and the newspapers, magazines and popular books give much the same mental habits to everyone. Questions are discussed from very much the same points of view, issues are presented in very much the same way; there is a striking sameness in the spirit of our novels, magazines and papers.

Of course it is not possible that any sameness of education or of intellectual impressions from sameness of literature should produce exactly the same sorts of minds. That is not claimed. I do maintain, with Spencer, that many of the conceptions of our fathers are not held by us to-day because of what might be called our intellectual *mood*. No specific arguments are forcing the older conceptions out of our churches, but a sort of mood makes it impossible to receive many of the older notions and to hold them as true. There is no reason why we should not believe in witches if we believe in the Bible, nor is there any reason for not believing in demon possession. Nevertheless, many who thoroughly believe in the Bible do not believe in these absurdities. They cannot give you a really good argument why, but the simple reason is that such beliefs are not in accord with the intellectual mood of to-day, even among the rigidly orthodox.

The results of Bible scholarship and the mood referred to have undoubtedly done some harm, yet every fair-minded observer must acknowledge that this newer Bible scholarship has made it impossible to hold to some of the peculiar interpretations of the Bible upon which a number of Sects have built, and also make it impossible to champion certain practices. No young minister with an honest mind who has carefully studied in the light of present-day scholarship could ever think of the Bible as maintaining and defending any doctrine of Church Polity, Close Communion or Apostolic Succession. The old methods of argument and contention are now inef-

spread of church unity. When thousands of young people meet in their great national meetings and share each other's Christian aspirations it is sheer folly to inject anything sectarian; it would not be tolerated. These young people do not ask each other, " What denomination do you belong to?" but rather, " What is your Society doing? Have you any new ideas to give us?" It is very easy for anyone brought up in such societies to pass from one denomination to another. The earnestness of these young Christians is doing a great deal toward breaking down the barriers between the churches.

The Sunday-school is a great leveller. Children of very different types of mind and of emotion,—of very different types of human nature,—attend the same Sunday-schools. They grow up and grow into the church whose Sunday-school they have been attending. Their natural preferences are not considered, indeed they are hardly felt. A youth does not know what he wishes to do or to be, he does not understand himself. When his religious life awakens he is very apt to join the church with which his parents are connected. As the majority of the members in any church come from the Sunday-school it is obvious that the Sunday-school is a means of the very first importance in bringing people of very unlike temperaments into the same church.

The exchange of church letters between different denominations helps to break down artificial barriers, but it is not a practice which makes entirely for uniformity. In such a country as ours where the population is constantly growing and shifting, there is a great deal of changing from one church to another. Often a member will take his church letter and join some church which appeals to his type of religious nature. This tends to strengthen church types.

A better spirit among clergymen is helping to bring a uniformity into the churches. Ministers' meetings where men of different creeds meet and exchange ideas, help to broaden their sympathies and bring the churches closer together. The habits of exchanging pulpits, of uniting services during the summer, of coöperating in civic work, all make for a better feeling and a closer sympathy between the churches.

Where there is coöperation between the official boards of different denominations, as, for example, in some Home Mission Boards, there is the best sign of a genuine move toward church federation. It is a great pity that no widespread national coöperation between the boards of the different denominations has yet been started.

As a whole, the gravitation toward unity of Christian life and thought makes itself felt more in the ranks of the Church than among the officers. In the laymen is the great hope. It is natural that pastors and secretaries of boards should give their efforts to the work immediately in hand and should lose sight of the greater work of Christianity as a whole. Denominational leaders are very slow to see the need of their going out of office in order to give place to great leaders representative of all Christianity. It is very difficult for a secretary in some one sect to see the necessity of his office going out of existence in order to merge his work into the work of Christianity as a whole. Undoubtedly, many men are Christians in heart who cling to their means of a livelihood at the expense of progress towards church unity. Unfortunately, the great leaders in the Church are not leading toward unity. Occasionally we hear pronouncements to the effect, " Our denomination stands for unity, we have always been desirous of church unity; we open our arms to receive all into our fold." This sounds hypocritical to a plain man. It is all "come to us." There is not even a frank willingness to compromise differences. These evasions give the colour of Christian breadth and charity, but they are more misleading than positive opposition. At heart many church leaders abhor union. Among those of their own profession, they acknowledge their prejudices and defend them by urging the peculiar worth of their variety of Christianity. This would be well enough if they acknowledged that the peculiar worth of their variety lay in the fact that there are temperamental differences in religious natures and their church answers certain natural needs. This would be honest and would open the way to coöperation, for it would acknowledge that church differences are based on human differences, and would escape the old superstition that each sect is peculiarly the child of God.

Not the least obstacle is a fear of something like church socialism. Great buildings, valuable sites, wealthy churches, large and successful publication houses and a number of other interests, it is feared would all have to go into a great melting pot, out of which fusion should come the future church. It is, however, a mere bogey. No such movement is necessary, or probable. The trend toward church unity will work out a much simpler and more effective method of coöperation. Nevertheless, the force of public opinion is undoubtedly the force which must bring about the coöperation between Sects and whatever of unity shall be achieved. Something of this sort is actually being accomplished. Social pressure is bringing the churches closer together.

Indeed, this is where each individual should put forth his efforts. Let each one seek to spread the conviction that the sects are an evil and menace the life of the Church, that coöperation, and not competition, must be the active spirit in Christianity. Then the soil is prepared for the spread of the great movement, when at length it shall get under way. Public opinion may be cultivated and prepared to receive certain conceptions just as the soil may be prepared to receive certain plants. Every sociologist knows that the spread of different fashions as well as different beliefs depends upon the social soil.

In studying the principles which seem to govern the spread of the Church in society some very interesting things come to light. One of these is the curious fact that the kind of public opinion which permits the spread of divorce is the kind of public opinion which also fosters Christian Science. Now, Christian Science does not cause divorce necessarily, and certainly divorce does not cause Christian Science. They are no more related than the pine and the scrub oak, but both pine and scrub oak flourish in the same soil. In comparing the spread of the social custom and a religious faith it is impossible to make comparisons of large sections of the country. Thus a state may have many Christian Science followers in the Protestant population and also have such a large number of Roman Catholics that its divorce rates will be very small; on the other hand, a state may have a high divorce rate but if it has very few cities it will have comparatively few Christian Science churches. The only safe comparison is between cities, and even here the figures are for the city and the county in which the city is situated, for divorce rates;

LEVELLING FORCES

while for Christian Science membership the figures are for the cities only. However, the city usually has such a large proportion of the population of its county that the remainder living only in the county is negligible. The following eighteen cities have been selected because they had a number of Christian Science churches in them and are representative of different portions of the country. New York, which occupies several counties, itself, is left out; and Boston, which is the centre of Christian Science, is also left out.

18 Cities arranged in order of largest number of Christian Science per 100,000 population	18 Cities arranged in order of the largest numbers of divorces. 100,000 in county containing city
Kansas City, Mo.	Kansas City, Mo.
Minneapolis	Indianapolis
Denver	Denver
Indianapolis	St. Joseph
Portland	Minneapolis
St. Joseph, Mo.	(Chicago) same rate
Cleveland	(Toledo) for both
Chicago	Portland
Toledo	(Cleveland) same rate
St. Paul, Minn.	(Detroit) for both
Buffalo	St. Louis
Detroit	Milwaukee
Milwaukee	Cincinnati
St. Louis, Mo.	St. Paul
Cincinnati	Baltimore
Richmond	Philadelphia
Baltimore	Buffalo
Philadelphia	Richmond

In the first six cities in each column five are the same and in the last six cities of each column four are the same; so at the head and at the foot of each list we find the same cities. If these results are studied carefully it

will be found that they can hardly be due to chance.*
Here then is an instance where public opinion, the social
conscience, makes possible or impossible the diffusion
of a given practice or faith.

If the educated Christians of this nation began to
address themselves to the great necessity of union among
the denominations the sentiment would spread first in
the cities. City churches of great strength and noble
reputation would become centres of the new movement;
just as the great cities in ancient times became the rallying points in the growth of Christianity. The movement would spread easily in some sections of the country and slowly in other sections. Its spread would depend upon the enlightenment and earnestness of the
laymen.

*C. C. Spearman: "Footrule for Measuring Correlation," *Brit. Jour. of Psychol.*, 2, pp. 89-108.

XIV

POSSIBILITIES AND IMPOSSIBILITIES IN CHURCH UNION

A VAST church of thirty million members has infinite possibilities. Nothing could stand the impact of its attack. The momentum of such an immense army would carry everything before it. In a decade deep-seated abuses would be swept out of the nation, in two generations there would not be a town or tribe the world around which would not live under the shadow of the cross. The present horde of sects marching in every direction with no concerted efforts would become an irresistible army, with a continuous firing line, with every camp in order and definite plan of campaign. Each individual church would have a place to fill, a work to do, and it would feel that its efforts were counting. This union of forces would keep the singleness of purpose throughout Christendom in prominence. Petty dissensions would dissolve and disappear in the heat of great achievements. The spirit of Christ would rest as sunlight upon all human lives. Surely, the inspiration of such a conception should fire men with a zeal for its realization.

Already there are movements toward church union; the term "Church Unity" is becoming familiar. There is considerable vagueness in the use of the term. Church union may mean a unity which imposes the same government, doctrines, worship and practical activities upon all the constituent churches. It may mean, also, the voluntary association of different sects for certain purposes, such as civic work, or mission work, or the founding of educational institutions. This latter is rather a federation of churches than a union.

Unity is possible to many denominations, federation is possible to all. If churches of widely unlike temperaments unite they are practically sure to separate eventually. Such a calamity would set back the sentiment of church unity a whole generation. To try to merge people whose church life is full of feeling with those cooler tempered doctrinaires would be to invite dissension. When the life of a church is seen, in the light of its past history and its present interests and practices, to have a certain definite tendency, it is obviously absurd to try to direct this tendency in a direction not congenial to it. At the present time there is no little danger that several denominations moved by very proper impulses may form a union. Overtures for such a union are already under way. The past of these sects has been quite different and the levelling influences at work upon them have not yet reduced them to a sufficient homogeneity. They could reshape their creeds and refashion their polities, but it is hardly possible that they would reshape their religious temperaments. Before a thoroughgoing unity is attempted the first step should be a federation. This would enable the work of each church to proceed without hindrance and at the same time would avoid unnecessary friction. As the churches understood each other better, as their pulpits would call the ministers of other sects in the federation, and as members would pass easily from one sect to another the temperamental differences would either become understood and allowance made for them, or they would gradually disappear; in the latter case genuine church unity is possible. A federation of some sort is possible among practically all of the sects. It should start with a frank recognition of differences. An honest consideration of the differences in mode of worship and life would quickly make clear that the issues between the churches do not go back to God but to human nature. As soon as men realize that their church has succeeded in a peculiar way, not because God has peculiarly favoured it and ignored others, but because it has met the particular needs of certain types of men, the attitude toward other churches will be vastly improved. We need to recognize that the very first disciples were not men of one type and that Christ never tried to make John like Peter, though He loved them both.

More specifically, what is the present situation? What can be done at the present time to further the unity of the churches? Obviously some things are practical and easily possible while other things are entirely out of the question.

Perhaps the first and easiest achievement would be the reunion of those sects within sects mentioned in an earlier chapter. The old issue of slavery is long since dead and there is no justification for Northern and Southern branches in the same denomination. If the Baptist, Methodist and Presbyterian churches would heal these old schisms, it would be a splendid step toward bringing all the denominations together. When the Southern States seceded, one set the example and the others followed in quick imitation. Imitation is a social force of great power. Could these great denominations show the world how differences may be forgotten, how problems of administration may be solved, and how unity can be achieved, their success would inspire many other similar efforts. As matters stand now the old issue lives on to the detriment of the whole Christian Church.

The possibility of bringing sects together which differ because of *national heritage* is much more difficult. These national churches carry with them the impetus of past traditions. Especially is this so in the churches in smaller communities and in the country. Time will wear down these differences and make church unity possible. But in the meantime the strategic years for spreading Christianity in foreign lands are slipping past. It would certainly be practicable for the larger churches in the great cities to start a movement toward federation and to seek true federation, to infuse a spirit of unity throughout their own sects. A number of intelligent and capable laymen in each sect could spread a sentiment which would make the future union of churches easier. It is not necessary to change doctrines and worship, but only the spirit of distrust. That must be changed. It should not be hard to work for the spread of Christianity independent of sect interests. Only a few men would resist such a church movement; for the average man is willing to believe in the genuineness of his neighbour's religion whether he be of the same national stock or not.

Racial differences are much harder to manage. Frankness and fair dealing will accomplish a great deal toward overcoming friction between different races in the Christian church. As Christianity spreads over the world different races must come together. What shall be the relation of one to the other? There is no place for race hatred in Christianity. Every genuine Christian is willing to coöperate with his brother in spreading civilization. There is no need for attempting to bring race tastes together. Where the races naturally gravitate together there is no problem, but where they gravitate toward different centres it is possible only to have a federation and not a union.

Such differences as those that appear between the Roman Catholic and the Protestant churches depend in no small measure upon differences of religious type. Often it is not a question of types, but of doctrine and worship so unlike that the very purpose of the church is distinct. If Protestantism means imitating Christ in character and conduct, simply using the Church as a means to accomplish this end, if Catholicism means the identification of an individual with an organization and the acceptance of its particular sacraments, then the purpose of these two great bodies is the same only in ethical issues. In these they may act together; but in the spread of their beliefs there is, at present, little hope for federation. However, with the increase of education even these barriers may be lowered so that some sort of coöperation may be possible.

The doctrinal differences which characterize a number of sects in the Protestant Church are not so dangerous as is often imagined. Creeds to-day are not the serious hindrance to unity that they were in the past. If the *laymen* of the Protestant churches were to write their beliefs down in black and white it would soon be seen that there are not sufficiently great differences to warrant different sects. It is the work of the specialist, the doctrinaire, which does the harm. Men who know no more about doctrinal matters than did the immediate followers of Christ can easily get together and work together.

With the sameness of viewpoint which characterizes educated men to-day, and with the desire for practical achievement which characterizes Americans, a platform of doctrinal unity could readily be drawn up by capable and devout laymen.

Church polity is not an insuperable barrier. Though it makes unity difficult it does not render federation impossible. As a matter of fact, a century's experience in different church polities has shown that each has its value and each has its defects. Probably no church is unwilling to make certain modifications for the better in its polity. Certainly few laymen would insist on their churches' polity at the expense of Christianity. Resistance to changes in polity comes largely from the office-holders, and this resistance would soon disappear in the presence of an earnest, determined movement for unity.

The great problem, indeed the greatest problem of all, is how to bring different natural types of religious experience together. It is obviously impossible to mix people who are naturally incompatible. Though differences which stand out rather conspicuously in church government, doctrines and practices may be ignored, the subtle differences of temperament and disposition which are often much less conspicuous cannot be ignored. From the study in the preceding chapters it is possible to map out very roughly what religious bodies might be expected to enter into more intimate relations with each other.

If the reader will turn back to page 201 and study the natural groups of the sects, it will be seen that, so far as the nature of the religious life is concerned, the partitions which have been thrown up around the various sects can easily be broken down, and from the remains a few large denominational walls may be erected. It is not necessary that any high sectarian walls should be raised, but it is very natural; and if they are to be erected at all, let them be erected along lines of natural differences. Such natural differences show very clear as one reads across the table.

The first thing which catches the attention in a study of this table is that the majority of the members of the Christian churches in America are found in those types which range from the emotional through the dogmatic into the intellectual. Here we probably have an American type. From this great central type others reach out in two directions, one towards a conversional type, which merges into that peculiar nature which is so susceptible to suggestion, that in turn fades into the impulsive and imitative type; in the other direction this central type leads off into altruistic and intellectual types.

The problem of assorting these various religious bodies is not a simple one. Of course they are all related, but the question of their similarities and dissimilarities is an exceedingly difficult one. Indeed, they overlap in so many places that the selection of a group for some one set can be made with no great certainty. However, if one begins to study the table in the upper left-hand corner and slowly reads across through the groupings of the sects down to the lower right-hand corner, a conviction will certainly arise maintaining the obvious unity of large groups of these sects. The Roman Catholic Church falls very largely in that class which may be instinctive and imitative, though its membership spreads through nearly all of the types. The Catholic Church in this country is undergoing many changes, the levelling influences have not succeeded in bringing this sect sufficiently into the spirit of modern times, as yet, for it to become soluble in any large merger of the denominations; this church, therefore, must stand in a group by itself.

The coloured churches with a preponderance of the emotional and convertible types have also their insoluble features which have been discussed. They may well constitute another group.

The next sect is that which has been so much discussed, the Christian Science. Probably this sect will be absorbed into the others in time; for the great source of strength which the other sects possess is denied to it; that is, the Sunday-school, which builds up a normal, healthy religious life and supplies recruits to the church, has no proper function in Christian Science. The membership is largely composed of those who have been members of other churches and have been drawn to Mrs. Eddy's doctrines after they had already become Christians. When the lesson of the Christian Science Church has been learned by the others, it will no longer have any *raison d'être*.

The next two sects whose types run well into the suggestible and convertible are the Methodists and Evangelical Association. The emphasis of these sects is upon spiritual experience, the faith and the life they develop should bring these two sects together. The Methodist includes more types than does the Evangelical Association. Many people in the Baptist churches could be equally comfortable in the Methodist, though the limits of these two sects among the different types do not coincide.

Inasmuch as the Baptist denomination includes men of the dogmatic and intellectual types it might be advisable to group another lot of denominations with the Baptists; that is, denominations which are composed of about the same types as those entering into the Baptist churches. Among these types are the Adventists, the Christian Connection, the Disciples of Christ, the Churches of Christ, the Dunkards, the Conservative Friends and the United Brethren. All of these sects have a large majority in their memberships which are of very much the same religious nature. There is more diversity of type in the Baptist churches than there is between the average Baptist and the average member of the other denominations in this group.

Another large group might well be headed by the Presbyterian churches. Here, too, there are a number of different types ranging from the dogmatic in which intellect and emotion are interlocked, through the altruistic to the dominantly intellectual. In this spread of types the Lutherans may easily find a place, though a minority of the Lutherans certainly runs out into the emotional types. Their adherence to their theoretical tenets proclaims their kinship to the Presbyterians. The Protestant Episcopal Church is composed of many people of exactly the same type as those in the Congregational and Presbyterian sects. President Charles Cuthbert Hall once declared that he had been amazed to find so many people who had been Presbyterians now in the Episcopal fold. In the Congregationalist we have a type very close to the more liberal wing of the Presbyterian Church. Ministers and members of Congregational churches pass into the Presbyterian churches very often and very easily.

Truly this gathering of Congregationalists, Episcopalians, Lutherans and, let us dare to add, Latter-day

Saints, looks like a combination which would result in an explosion rather than in a cement. That, however, is a superficial estimate of this group. Beneath the differences in ecclesiastical vestments are members of the same family. What deceives the eye is the outward appearance, and truly the outward appearances of these sects are very dissimilar! But within we find people of the same great types; people of the same tastes and abilities in other courses of life. Great partitions are those between these sects, but they are not formidable; once down, the sects themselves would find the majority of their members very congenial fellow-worshippers. This applies, of course, to the native Americans in the Lutheran churches. As for the Latter-day Saints their tenets will probably exclude them from uniting with any other denominations for some time to come; nevertheless, the average man in that sect is not unlike the average member of a Western Congregational, Presbyterian or Lutheran Church. Some of the members of the Friends and the Dunkers might well go into this group, while the less progressive wings of those two sects might find a more comfortable home in that group which the Baptist denomination heads.

The Unitarian and the Universalist churches are so evidently similar and so thoroughly of the intellectual type that they might easily unite into one body. This would be a very becoming and proper performance, as both of these sects have been leaders in many matters. Why should they not lead in practical church unity?

Though these groups have in them sects which from a theoretical point of view are not even first cousins and whose polities are not to be found on the same family tree, nevertheless the *people* who make up the sects are of one parentage. It is the nearness of type rather than doctrine which establishes a unity that can endure. We have seen many instances of the same doctrine and the same polity spreading up into factions. Unity is not to be found in any artificial similarity.

These bodies, the Catholic as one great division, the Afro-American churches as another, the Methodist and Evangelical Association as a third, the Baptist and their affiliated bodies as a fourth, the Presbyterian and its affiliated bodies as a fifth, and the Unitarian and the Universalist constituting the sixth, would have within their walls over thirty-one million members. Such a vast church, or rather such vast churches, could sway the world. I said at first such a church, for I am convinced that these great groups, formed because of their natural similarities of spiritual nature, would not act as independent churches but as branches of one vast church. When men can bring themselves to believe that the church to which they belong owes its existence as a separate sect not to any act of God, but to a natural preference of men, then the attitude of distrust and suspicion disappears. Sympathy and fellowship appear. No artilleryman would claim that the artillery defends the country more efficiently than the battleship. No cavalryman claims his superiority to the marine in the defense of his country or in its esteem. All these are branches of one great common cause. Each man serves his country where his talent and ability best fit; it is talent and ability which determine his place,—human preference, not divine. So in the army of God, let the human dispositions be frankly recognized and every member of the Christian church will see the whole body of his fellow-worshippers in their true perspective; there will be no "*chosen of God,*" for all will be equally chosen of God. It is impossible to hope that this frame of mind will become common in the very near future, it is something which education alone can bring about. Once it is achieved church unity will be accomplished easily.

Could a series of great sects be formed, based on their natural similarities, many of the obstacles to the progress of Christianity would disappear. Among them would go that oft-heard criticism, "What is Christianity? What church is really the Christian church?" The spirit of competition which is the curse of the churches in so many small towns and villages, would necessarily fade away and the attitude of suspicion, almost of hostility, would give place to a far better spirit. These advantages are nothing like so great as the tremendous advantage of administering the wealth and strength of Christianity in such a way that Christ's cause is advanced and not impeded. In the present age the advantage which looms largest lies in the mission fields. Here some sort of unity is simply indispensable.

In the *Report of Commission VIII on Coöperation and Promotion of Unity for the World's Missionary Conference, 1910,* the demand for unity cannot fail to impress even the most casual observer of church affairs. The Report shows that in China, Japan, India and Africa many conferences have been held among representatives of different sects. These conferences were the outgrowth of general needs. They often covered large sections of the mission fields. So great is the difference between Christianity and the heathen people that the microscopic differences between Christians disappear for everyone but the most near-sighted and narrow-minded sectarian. "For the accomplishment of this overwhelming task it

CHURCH UNION

seems essential that the Christian church should present a united front. Its divisions are a source of weakness and impair the effectiveness of its testimony to the one gospel of the Son of God which it professes. The issues are so great that there can be no trifling in the matter. The evangelizing of nations, the Christianizing of empires and kingdoms, is the object before us. The work has to be done now. It is urgent and must be pressed forward at once. The enterprise calls for the highest qualities of statesmanship and for the maximum efficiency in all departments of work. It is not surprising that those who are in the front of this great conflict and on whose minds and souls the gravity of the issues presses most immediately, should be the first to recognize the need for concerted action and closer fellowship" (p. 131). What a shame it is that the work of Christ should be impaired by those who are endeavouring to further it because of artificial differences in church polity and in historical creeds. "It is evident that so long as missionaries are sent out and controlled by missionary societies in Western lands, and the churches planted by them maintain connection with these home societies, movements toward unity in the mission field cannot proceed far without the coöperation and support of those responsible for missionary administration at home. Several of our correspondents state quite emphatically that the chief difficulty in the way of effective coöperation has been the lack of support on the part of societies at home. Further, it is obvious that since the missionaries working in any particular area of the mission field often belong to different nationalities, coöperation at the home base to be effective in all cases must be not only of an interdenominational but also of an international character" (p. 119).

Some definite steps could be taken at once in the direction of church coöperation in foreign lands. If the groups of churches mentioned above could decide that they would act together in the spreading of the gospel, it would be altogether practicable to plan their missionary combination and direct the advance of Christianity with great efficiency. One very practical movement might be set afoot at once. There is no great centre for all mission activity. Such a centre could well be established, every denomination coöperating. Our missionaries go into foreign lands not knowing the language they are to use, often not understanding the people they are to meet, frequently having no idea of what sort of preparation is necessary. It requires years for them to overcome these handicaps. An institution should be endowed which would enable those determining to give their lives to missions to spend several years in direct preparation for a certain work in a certain field. This institution should be the centre of missionary interests for every denomination. With it, every mission board should coöperate; and every theological seminary should be in close touch with it. Here, missionaries who have laboured for years could bring the treasures of their experiences. Years of mistaken effort would be avoided by a few years' working in such an institution. In the place of the regular theological course given to those who intend to be pastors in our own country there would be courses in preparation for active work in mission fields. It would be possible for the mission Boards to determine, if they acted in coöperation, into what fields they would send new missionaries. This would enable anyone determining to devote his life to missionary work to prepare for work in some particular line. Its language could be

CHURCH UNION

acquired, the traits of its people could be studied, the needs of the country could be learned. The man who went into a field knowing what was needed would undoubtedly have some practical knowledge at his disposal based on the needs of the people, for different countries are appealed to in different ways. He would know something about agriculture and agricultural implements and would be in a position to carry some of the modern advantages of our civilization; he would carry with him a knowledge of some of the sciences which are indispensable to our age. In short, instead of filling his hours of preparation with useless information about creeds and dogmas and church history and dead languages, he would fill his time with a preparation which would apply directly to his work.

From such a centre as this, to which all Christian churches contributed, would flow in return an inspiration for Christian fellowship and Christian service which cannot be measured.

A large program has been mapped out; perhaps someone will substitute the word "visionary" for "large." All great accomplishments are visionary before they are accomplished. After their achievement they are said to be in line with the natural evolution of civilization and inevitable. Two things are inevitable, either a great calamity in the churches, and a so-called Christian civilization losing its one great faith and following other peoples in a division of faiths, or the native strength and spirit of American Christianity may rise above the difficulties which beset it and prepare itself for greater efforts. The strategic years are slipping away. What is to be done must be done quickly. No mistake will be made if those denominations whose religious natures are closely akin break down the ancient walls and rebuild along the lines of least natural resistance. This would give six or eight great denominations. These are all for which any justification can be found. There is absolutely not one word of defense for sectarianism apart from the natural differences in human beings. When these differences are frankly recognized and every man worships God in his own way, recognizing that it is his own way, then the dawn of the new era has begun. No greater mistake can be made than to attempt to unite church sects that are naturally far apart. Indeed, the natural separation which one sees in the Dunkards, the Friends, the Disciples and a number of others, is a separation which must be recognized frankly. These great groups would allow just such differences of type as those which cause such separations. There might easily be a changing from one large group to another on the part of those who find themselves out of sympathy with the denominations with which they are affiliated. No hard and fast lines can be drawn. Time alone can work out the best details, but in working out these details the large lines of differences in type of religious life must be observed.

XV

IN CONCLUSION

A FEW paragraphs are necessary in conclusion to correct certain misunderstandings which I believe are almost inevitable in a reading of the foregoing chapters.

In constantly insisting upon the physical basis of differences in temperament, and, therefore, in religion, it is very easy to lose sight of the spiritual character of religion itself. Several works have appeared in Religious Psychology in which the avowed intent was to assist religious people in an understanding of their religious lives, but which unfortunately left their readers with the impression that religion can be analyzed in terms of *nerve action!* Nothing could be further from the truth. It is the conviction of the author that what the old theologians called the Holy Spirit is an actual working reality in the world of man. This conviction has not been defended in this work, as it would be out of place here. What has been said may be accepted by the Theist or by the Atheist, as it has had to do with observable facts. The chief question at issue has been how the sects have been formed and sustained. This question has called for Sociology and Psychology, but not for Theology. To revert to an old figure; the lilies with their stems reaching into the black earth at the bottom of the pond and lifting their white petals above the green scum are alike, or they are different, because of the materials from which they are built and not because of the life-giving sunlight which rests upon them. It is the same divine spirit which enters into all religion, but it is conditioned by the nature into which it enters.

Another sort of misunderstanding may well arise in a book of this character. Many books consist of close-knit arguments; break one of these links and the whole work falls to pieces. That is not so of this work. Many an error may creep in unobserved, but the central truths remain unaltered. For example, the grouping of the sects probably is not correct in all details, but the fact that *the sects differ in nature and that some are closer together than others* still remains.

This is not intended as a text-book. It is pioneer work. It seeks to do nothing more than to blaze a trail. It does not boast that the surveyor who comes after will find all the lines straight, but it does maintain that its general direction is true and that its final destination is sure. No book can begin to cover all the ground which the preceding chapters have touched upon. To do full justice to every phase of the subjects treated a series of volumes would be necessary. Among the details of the chapters the one central truth for which the book is written may be obscured. May one closing word make that truth stand forth!

Never has there been a sect made by God.

Every group of worshippers has been drawn together by influences which may be explained naturally.

If the sects were social or political bodies these influences would be acknowledged instantly. But among religious bodies such social and psychological principles are obscured. However, this very obscuration is easily explained. No man with a fair mind and with an average education can read of the formation and the perpetuation of the sects and still cling to the superstition that they are the work of God. Clear and unmistakable is the evidence that human nature alone made and maintains the sects,—in religion. Obviously and incontrovertibly the perpetuation of the sects is a menace to Christianity itself. No greater satisfaction can come to the author than to know that these pages have done something, however small, to bring to realization the prayer of the Founder of our faith: "That they all may be one; as thou, Father, art in Me and I in Thee, that they also may be one in us, that the world may believe that Thou hast sent Me."

PRACTICAL CHRISTIANITY

HAROLD BEGBIE

Twice-Born Men
A Clinic in Regeneration.

12mo, cloth, net 50

A footnote in narrative to Prof. Wm. James' "The Varieties of Religious Experience."

Studies in the phenomena of conversion from the standpoint of the student of human nature.

Prof. William James, of Harvard: "Mr. Begbie's book is a wonderful set of stories splendidly worked up. It certainly needs no preface from me. I might as well call my book a foot-note to his. I am proud of the dedication and of the references and I wish the book a great success."

Prof. George A. Coe, of Union Theological Seminary: "I like the book greatly. It gives concrete data and that is what both the psychologist and religionist needs. As I read, I found myself marking the margins and singling out passages for my own scientific use."

JAMES I. VANCE

Tendency: The Effect of Trend and Drift in the Development of Life.

Net $1.25.

A series of discussions of formative influences in character construction, from a practical and sympathetic standpoint. Dr. Vance's work among young men enables him to speak authoritatively. To this he adds insight and sympathy.

SIR JOSEPH COMPTON-RICKETT

Origins and Faith

8vo, cloth, net $1.50.

A series of essays, philosophical and theological, written by this eminent statesman and layman on the fundamentals of belief. It is a frank examination and apologetic for Christianity, by one who is well known now as the author of the erstwhile anonymous books "The Christ That is to Be" and "Pro Christo et Ecclesia."

EDWIN F. HALLENBECK

The Passion for Men

16mo, cloth. net 40c.

A series of straightforward talks on the imperative duty of soul winning, by the recent associate pastor of the Fifth Avenue Presbyterian Church, New York.

THE CHURCH AND ITS WORK

HENRY C. McCOMAS, Ph.D.

The Sects

A Comparison of Religious Types. Cloth, net $1.25.

A study of the origin of the various denominations. When and how did they begin? Is there real need for one hundred and eigthy odd sects in America or are they a positive hindrance to the Church? The scientific spirit is in evidence throughout these chapters but so, also is the spirit of reverence. The book is constructive not iconoclastic.

CHARLES STELZLE

American Social and Religious Conditions

Illustrated with numerous charts and tables. 12mo, cloth, net

This work may be used both as a text book for study classes and for general reading. It contains the findings of the Men and Religion Surveys in seventy principal cities, of which the author had charge. Mr. Stelzle also served as the dean of the Social Service throughout the Movement. Out of a wide and practical experience in City Work the author discusses a program for the Church, especially with regard to the "down-town" situation. The book contains many original charts and diagrams.

CHARLES S. MACFARLAND

Spiritual Culture and Social Service

12mo, cloth, net $1.00.

A stirring call to service. Dr. Macfarland, as pastor of Congregational churches in large industrial centres, has had first hand experience in some of the most pressing problems now confronting the church. As secretary of the Social Service Commission of the Council of Churches of Christ in America, he is now engaged in solving the problem in a larger way. He has a message to deliver and he presents it with a force and conviction that cannot fail to deeply impress and influence the reader.

ARTHUR V. BABBS, A.B.

The Law of the Tithe

As Set Forth in the Old Testament. 12mo, cloth, net $1.50.

"A book of very genuine scholarship—a complete history of the universality of the tithe—the ablest and perhaps the most interesting explanation of this ancient custom that has appeared."—*N. Y. Christian Advocate.*

CONCERNING FOREIGN LANDS

ARTHUR E. COPPING

A Journalist in the Holy Land

Profusely Illustrated in Colors by Harold Copping, F.R.A. 8vo, cloth, net $2.00.

The *London Times* says: "This is just what one would expect from the collaboration of a genial and clever journalist and an accomplished artist." The *Scotsman* says: "Mr. Copping's story is graphically told with many humorous touches and especially noteworthy for its human interest in the existing inhabitants of the country."

ROBERT H. MILLIGAN

Fetish Folk of West Africa

Illustrated, 12mo, cloth, net $1.50.

The author of that fascinating volume THE JUNGLE FOLK OF AFRICA has written another book on the dark continent which is every bit as interesting as the first. The author says, "Both are about the people of Africa, whatever interest they have is entirely human, but the first is observational, the second is more intimate, and studies the African from the standpoint of his beliefs—fetishism."

J. DYER BALL

Of the Hong Kong Civil Service Retired

The Chinese at Home

An Inside View of the Man of Tong and His Awakening. Illustrated, 12mo, cloth, net $2.00.

"Probably the most intimate study of the Chinaman ever given to the Western World replete with revelations of a people living for ages behind doors closed to 'the foreign devil', and the story is told most entertainingly. Mr. Ball speaks with authority, exploding one false idea after another and revealing to the eyes of the West the real China."—*N. Y. Times.*

W. A. P. MARTIN, D.D., LL.D.

The Lore of Cathay

Or, The Intellect of China. In five parts: Arts and Sciences, Literature, Philosophy and Religion, Education, History. By the former President of the Imperial University at Peking. *New Popular Edition.* Illustrated, net $1.50.

KIYOSHI K. KAWAKAMI, M. A.

American-Japanese Relations

An Inside View of Japan's Policies and Purposes. 8vo, cloth, net $2.00.

"Mr. Kawakami treats of these questions with vigor, clearness and judicial breadth of view.... The book is the ablest and most exhaustive on the theme.... The author threshes out the facts concerning Japanese immigration, coming to the same conclusion that scientific inquirers, the best business men and the statesmen, whose eyes are not on votes, have long held.... Mr. Kawakami's arguments are sound."
—*New York Times.*

HOME MISSIONS

LEMUEL C. BARNES, D.D.

Elemental Forces in Home Missions
12mo, cloth, net 75c.
By the author of that popular missionary text-book, "Two Thousand Years of Missions Before Carey." Some of the most important issues connected with the work of Christianizing America are presented with a breadth, a clearness, a force and a conviction that will give the reader a new vision of the Home Mission opportunity and a new sense of his responsibility.

JAMES F. LOVE, D.D.

Ass. Cor Sec Hom Mission Board Southern Baptist Convention

The Mission of Our Nation
12mo, cloth, net $1.00.
"Doctor Love shows himself at once a historian and a prophet as he opens the book of the past and points out its suggestion for the future. The reader is irresistibly carried forward to the conclusions of the author. Interesting, illuminating and inspiring."—*Baptist Teacher.*

MARY CLARK BARNES

Early Stories and Songs for New Students of English
Illustrated, 16mo, cloth, net 60c.; paper, net 35c.
Dr. Edward A. Steiner says: "Not only practical but it affords easy transition to the higher things. The Bible is a wonderful primer, simple, yet wonderfully profound. I am glad that it is the basis of your system of teaching English to foreigners."

HOME MISSIONS—TEXT BOOKS

BRUCE KINNEY, D.D.

Mormonism: The Islam of America
Home Mission Study Course. Illustrated, 12mo, cloth, net 50c.; paper, net 30c.
Dr. Kinney treats the subject in a judicious way, avoiding denunciation or undue criticism. The facts of Mormon history, doctrine and life are woven into a readable story that is sure to hold the attention.

JOHN R. HENRY

Some Immigrant Neighbors
The Home Mission Junior Text Book. Illustrated, 12mo, cloth, net 40c.; paper, net 25c.
The author is the pastor of "The Church of All Nations" in New York City. He writes of many nationalities from his own experience. Through his sympathetic portrayal the child student will be drawn toward a neighborly feeling for his little brothers of foreign speech.

Date Due